1·25

MOTOR CARS

1770 - 1940

MOTOR
CARS
1770 - 1940
Juraj Porázik

**Illustrations
Ján Oravec**

Cover illustration: Peter Hutton

*Front Cover: Ford Model A
Back Cover: Vauxhall Prince Henry*

Galley Press

English language edition, designed and produced by
Autumn Publishing Limited, Chichester, England

Published in this edition by Galley Press,
an imprint of W H Smith & Son Limited
Registered No. 237811 England.
Trading as WHS Distributors,
St John's House, East Street, Leicester LE1 6NE.

ISBN 0 86136 883 5

Translation Maria Jansova and Vladimir Sojak

© 1981 Slovart Publishers, Bratislava.

Typesetting by Avonset, Midsomer Norton, Bath.
Printed in Czechoslovakia.

HORSELESS CARRIAGES

The dream of self-propelling vehicles has been in Man's mind for centuries. Vehicles driven by men hidden inside them were built as early as the Middle Ages. In 1490 Leonardo da Vinci built a manpowered vehicle. Independently of James Watt, who developed the first steam engine in 1769, the first steam carriage of the Frenchman Nicolas Cugnot appeared in 1769-1770, followed by Richard Trevithick's mail coach (1801), Hancock's passenger steam carriage (1882), and a French omnibus in 1873. It was generally believed that steam was the appropriate driving force for self-propelling vehicles.

In the meantime another development was taking place. In 1806 a vehicle was built in the workshop of Isaac de Rivaz in the Swiss canton of Valais which could move for a few metres by using the power of an internal-combustion engine. The Frenchman Étienne Lenoir came up with the idea of mixing petrol gases with air and then using this mixture as a driving force. His simple engine powered a vehicle which was driven from central Paris to the suburb of Joinville-le-Pont.

In Cologne Nicolaus Otto had set up a small workshop in which he continued development of Lenoir's gas engine. During one of his experiments he came across some ideas which were basic to the development of the internal-combustion engine, such as compression of the air-fuel mixture in the combustion area, and the four-stroke cycle. Otto had the four-stroke cycle patented in 1876, not knowing then that the Frenchman Beau de Roscha had theoretically explained the principle of the four-stroke engine as early as 1862. Therefore after Roscha's heirs had sued Otto, the Reich Supreme Court cancelled Otto's patent and from then on anybody who wished to do so was free to manufacture four-stroke engines.

Otto's gas engine was followed by Gottlieb Daimler's light petrol engine suitable for powering vehicles. Daimler's 460 cc speed single-cylinder engine developed 1.1kW (1.5hp) at 700 rpm. The engine, called the 'Pendulum Clock' operated with surface ignition and was fitted with a surface-evaporation carburettor.

While Karl Benz was assembling his motorized three-wheeler in his Mannheim workshop in 1885, Daimler built the first motorcycle in the world. Having iron-tyred wooden wheels and a wooden frame, it weighed 90kg (198lb) and achieved a speed of 12km/h (7½mph). The 'Pendulum Clock' was cooled by a fan, and fitted in a frame with rubber joints. In the autumn of 1886 Daimler amazed his friends by the first four-wheeler fitted with a high-speed internal-combustion engine. The vehicle could maintain a speed of 18km/h (11mph). After the World Exhibition in Paris in 1889 nothing could stop the ever-increasing popularity of Benz' and Daimler's vehicles. In the following years the engine power kept steadily increasing to 15, 20, and even 45kW (20, 30, 60hp). The early belt drive was abandoned, and an automobile of a modern concept was evolved with a front-mounted engine followed by the clutch, the gearbox, the propeller shaft, and the differential. The engineers set their minds to determine the best bore and stroke ratio. They also pondered over the piston speed, the problems of cylinder filling, and other questions important in designing ever more efficient and, at the same time, more economical engines. At the turn of the century Bosch's magneto ignition was invented.

The brakes of the new, faster vehicles were relatively weak, and they soon became the main problem. In order to improve the efficiency of the hand-brake, vehicles were fitted with chocks that were quickly put down under the wheels when the vehicle had to stop on a gradient. As early as 1900 it was mandatory that every automobile be fitted with two brakes functioning independently. The pedal shoe-brake governed either the front or the rear wheels. The hand-brake gradually acquired the function of an auxiliary brake.

At first nobody gave a thought to electric lighting, since carbide illumination was available.

The first automobile events and races were a great incentive to technical development. The 1900 Gordon-Bennett Cup was the first race with strictly specified rules. The weight of the cars was limited to between 400 and 1000kg (880-2000lb).

Only four-seaters could be entered for the Herkomer trials, held from 1905 to 1907. The cars' equipment had to meet the motoring demands of the period. The vehicles were divided into classes according to their engine performance for the first time. Similar procedures were adopted in organizing the Prince Henry Trials. These competition rules influenced the choice of materials. Light metals were used for the first time. Among other novelties were ball bearings, mechanically controlled valves, multiple speed gearboxes, improved carburettors, and many other details which increased engine output and cruising speed. In 1906 the first Grand Prix events were held. This was an era of steadily growing application of the compressor principle in engine designing. Performances of powerful supercharged engines allowed the races to achieve what seemed then to be incredibly high speeds.

Apart from that, various motor works had been building vehicles of a wide range of designs. The most interesting of them will be dealt with in the following pages.

CHARACTERISTIC FEATURES

BODY

The first automobiles were, in fact, still carriages, without shafts and with an engine mounted beneath the seats. The development of carriage into motor car was also determined by the seat arrangement,

1893

1902

and by efforts to protect the passengers against harsh weather. The bodywork was either of a *Vis-à-Vis* type, that is with a face-to-face arrangements of seats, or *Dos-à-Dos* (back-to-back). Among other body types were landau, brake, and phaeton. In the early 20th century there were no fewer than 20 designs. Most of their names were French, because they were terms internationally used for carriage bodies.

1910

1915

After the classical design with engine in the front had pushed its way through at Mercedes Simplex, the basic body shape resembled more or less that of a modern vehicle. While cars were still largely hand built, coachwork depended on the craftsmanship of the bodybuilders. Wood, the traditional construction material, was gradually replaced by metal. Various bodies were fitted to handmade chassis. This was a period of boom in body designing, and it favoured the establishment of new firms which specialized in body styling.

The ever-increasing maximum speeds in the 1920s also affected

1927

1932

coachwork. The automobile was fitted with a wedge-shaped radiator, long mudguards connected to footboards, a slanting windshield, and compact side-walls.

The knowledge of the laws of aerodynamics affected body-styling of the early 1930s. The so-called streamline body accentuated speed. Ideal features appeared to be a car with a long bonnet, long steel mudguards, and a solidly elegant bodyline.

More compact engines made better use of space, giving more room for comfortable seats. The most important change concerned the classical chassis, which was replaced by a body shell. Switching to a body shell simplified production, cut down costs, and made volume production possible. The various modifications of bodywork are shown on the following pages.

1935

1939

WHEELS

The noisy iron-shod wheels of the first motor vehicles were hard and unaccommodating, and even the best springs could not prevent severe jolting. A wheel with a solid rubber tyre was an advanced feature in comparison with the iron wheels. Small bumps were absorbed, and the driver simply avoided the big ones.

The invention of tyres was of a great significance. In 1845 an Edinburgh businessman, William Thomson, claimed a patent on tyres, which were even used on carriages in London's Hyde Park. But his patent was forgotten.

In 1887 a Scottish veterinary surgeon, John Boyd Dunlop, bent a rubber hose, provided it with a valve of his own design, and glued the tyre to his son's tricycle. Riding a vehicle with inflated tyres proved much smoother, and left hardly any traces in the garden. Dunlop

obtained a patent on this tyre. However, despite the obvious advantages, this novelty also had a few drawbacks. The tyres slipped off the wheels and they were difficult to repair. This was particularly serious in racing, since people involved in it were much concerned about changing tyres in the shortest possible time.

In France, Édouard Michelin mounted Dunlop's tyres on the wheels of a Peugeot car, and with his brother entered for the first automobile race, Paris-Bordeaux-Paris. For this race he developed detachable rim flanges which were bolted to the wheel discs. During the race Michelin had to change flat tyres 65 times — but the advantages of the invention had been proved. He and his brother founded a tyre factory in Clermont-Ferrand and put an end to the import of British tyres to France. The development of the German tyre industry began with the establishment of the Continental Caoutchouc and Gutta-Percha Company in 1873, and later continued with the firms Metzeler and Peter.

Finally, the so-called Rudge-Whitworth wheels were developed in 1914. They were detachable wire-spoked wheels with a hub fastened by a central bolt. On racers and sports cars this bolt became a wingnut, which could be loosened with a hammer.

Today every car is fitted with detachable disc wheels with three, four, or five retaining bolts.

RADIATORS

Gottlieb Daimler's first high-speed car engine was air-cooled, but tests with water cooling were also under way. Car designers based one of the first water-cooling systems on the evaporation principle, to remove the heat of combustion from the engine. The steam thus produced was led through a cooling coil-labyrinth to a condenser and back to the tank.

In 1890 Gottlieb Daimler introduced a novelty. He let the water flow through the tubular frame of his *Stahlradwagen'*. Water circulation was provided by a pump placed between the engine and the tube system. Many designers, among them Franklin, Porsche, and de Dion, concentrated on a cooling system which is considered modern even by present-day standards. They fitted the front-mounted engine with ribs, and the flowing air stream performed the cooling function.

Today, a great many cars are equipped with thermo-syphon cooling, which is based on the circulation of cold and warm water. However, the most usual system is forced circulation cooling, in which circulation is provided by a small water pump. The typical honeycomb radiator, scaled down in the course of time, has remained a characteristic feature of many car trademarks, such as Rolls-Royce, Mercedes, Alfa-Romeo, BMW, and Cadillac.

The radiator grille was a matter of style in America. Oldsmobile realized that the radiator did not need to be silver-plated, and started using chrome on its models instead. The Opel brothers in Rüsselsheim, Germany, immediately followed the Americans.

HISPANO-SUIZA

ZEPPELIN

ROLLS ROYCE

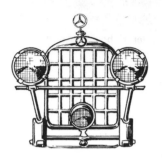

MERCEDES

ISOTTA-FRASCHINI

BUGATTI

VOISON

ALFA ROMEO

In the following decades the large radiators diminished to smaller, narrow cooling grilles, but everything was fundamentally the same under the bonnet. And it was only the clouds of steam, which were the typical feature of the oldtimers, that disappeared.

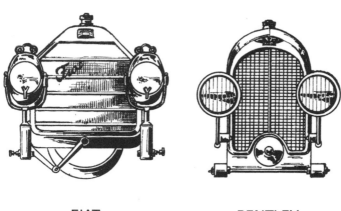

FIAT   BENTLEY

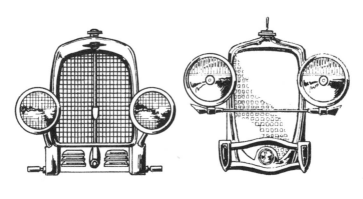

ASTON MARTIN   DUESENBERG

THE STEERING WHEEL

The first horseless carriages differed from their horse-drawn predecessors only by the tiller or lever used for the front-axle steering. Vehicles with these column-mounted levers looked strange, and were nicknamed 'coffee mills'. Gradually the steering column inclined backwards, and the lever was replaced by a steering wheel.

Steering an overloaded front axle was so difficult that at times all passengers had to give a hand. Vehicles with smaller front wheels were easier to control, even though every bend was a risk.

The carriage would have never turned into the car had the steering problem not been solved. In 1889 Daimler developed a steering system, used independently by Benz in 1893. The steering was designed so as to turn the front wheels through different radii, independently of one another. Finally, the traditional carriage shape was abandoned, and all wheels were the same size.

The driver's section of the first vehicles was fitted not only with the steering column, but also other controls, such as the transmission lever, the driving belt lever, a fuel-mixture regulator, manual accelerator, and an ignition-advance regulator.

The number of spokes in the steering wheel has continuously changed. Most early cars had four-spoke steering wheels. For a number of years it was only the French Renault which had a five-spoke steering wheel. The more sober European motor companies lingered behind in introducing the three-spoke steering wheel, which came into use in America in the late 1920s.

In the post Second World War period a two-spoke steering wheel was introduced and in 1955 Citroën designed its single spoke wheel. While maintaining its controlling function, the steering wheel has also turned into a distinctive feature of particular makes.

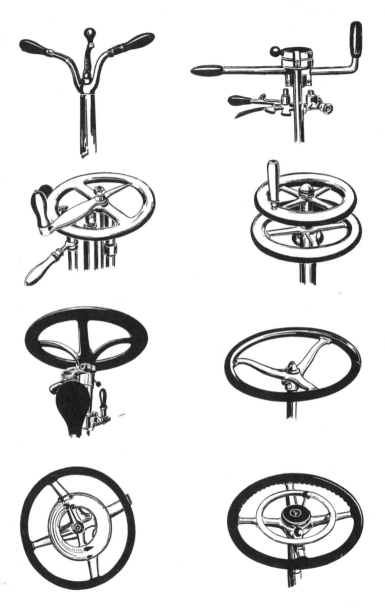

17

BENZ

Karl Benz was born in 1844 in Karlsruhe, Germany, the son of a railway mechanic. He studied for some time at the Karlsruhe Polytechnic, but he did not finish his studies and started working as a technician in a machine shop in Karlsruhe. However, Benz strove for financial independence, and at the age of 27 he set up, with partners, a workshop in Mannheim to develop his own internal-combustion engine. Benz's first engines were of a two-stroke design, as opposed to Otto's patented four-stroke. Benz's dream was to design a complete automobile. Since his business partners did not encourage his plans, he sold his shares in the company, and started afresh with a loan from a metal dealer, Max Rosel, and established Benz & Co, Rheinische Gasmotorenfabrik. These works finally provided Benz with the conditions necessary for designing and manufacturing his own car. Meanwhile, the validity of Otto's patent had been questioned. Benz improved the four-stroke; his version had high revolutions and weighed less than other engines, and was suitable to drive a car.

Benz's first car was a three-wheeler, with a single front wheel steered by a simple tiller. Benz introduced his first four-wheeler in 1893. This 'Victoria' model went into small-scale manufacture. His next model was the Velo, the forerunner of the later popular 'Comfortable'. Both vehicles were two-seaters.

In the early 1900s Benz & Co. failed financially, and in 1903 Benz left his Mannheim works. But new commercial success came in 1905 after the arrival of a young engineer, Hans Nibel, in the design department.

As a result of the post-war economic situation, Benz & Co. and Daimler Motorengesellschaft, merged on June 29, 1926, as the Daimler-Benz AG, and became a leading car producer.

BMW

The trademark BMW was created by the merger of two companies in Munich, which were mainly engaged in making aircraft engines: BFW, which stands for Bayerische Flugzeugwerke AG, established in 1916, and Rapp-Motoren-Werke, established in 1913. The boom in the aircraft industry during the First World War increased the volume of Rapp's production, and this led to the firm becoming a joint stock company, BMW GmbH. Its initial capital came from Camillo Castiglioni, a banker from Vienna. After conclusion of the Versailles Treaty, which stopped Germany making armaments, both companies searched for substitute production. BFW produced motorcycles and office furniture. BMW received an order to manufacture Knorr air brakes. On May 20, 1922, Castiglioni became the owner of both companies. The new works in Munich were renamed the Bayerische Motoren Werke AG. The blue and white trademark symbolizes a revolving airscrew, an echo of the firms' origins.

The start of car development dates from 1922, when designer Max Fritz introduced a new air-cooled flat twin-cylinder engine. It was designed for stationary work, but it was also used in motorcycles and cars. Actual car production did not begin until 1928, when BMW was sold to Dixi Werke in Eisenach, where at that time the Austin Seven was being produced under licence. It was followed by the AM 4, and in 1934 the 315 model, with a six-cylinder engine, was manufactured. In 1936 the 326 model was fitted with a new radiator grille, which has not changed since. Noteworthy features of this car were the torsion-bar-sprung rear axle, and the fully synchromesh gearbox. The 327, a beautiful convertible version, was derived from the 326, using a 2-litre engine developing 40kW (55bhp), followed by the most popular sports car, the 328.

Post Second World War production commenced with the 501 model, followed by 502 and 503. Finally a stylish 507 sports model, fitted with the first German V8 engine with a capacity of 3168 cc, developing 110kW (150bhp), was announced.

The success of BMW, which has maintained its popularity, rests on the excellent quality and steady improvement of its remarkable designs.

BUGATTI

The success of the Bugatti trademark coincides with the achievements of Ettore Bugatti, a genius of world car industry. He was born on September 15, 1881, in Milan, the son of a painter. He designed cars in Alsace as a subject of the German emperor, and finally became a citizen of the French Republic. But he still considered himself an Italian.

At the age of 20 Bugatti introduced his first car at a show in Milan. His vehicle drew the attention of the business world, and the De Dietrich works of Niederbronne, in Alsace, engaged Bugatti and obtained a licence to manufacture his car. Since he was too young to sign a contract, he concluded the deal through his father. In this factory he designed a number of popular models, such as the Peugeot Bébé and the Mathis Hermes. He offered some of his designs to the Gasmotorenfabrik Deutz AG.

After his initial success, Bugatti struck out on his own. He was 30 when he and his partners began building cars at Molsheim, in Alsace. His first production car was called 'Type 13' and in spite of this unlucky number its drivers did extremely well on the track. With the small 1.3-litre Bugatti 13 Ernest Friedrich humbled a big Fiat driven by Hemery in the Le Mans Grand Prix. Altogether 205 cars of the Type 13 model, fitted with an OHC engine, were manufactured.

After the First World War Alsace became part of France and Bugatti a French subject. A racing version of the Type 13 was introduced, the 22/23 model, which won the first four places in the 1921 Brescia Grand Prix. From then on the Bugatti Brescia model spread the fame of the Molsheim works.

In the early 1920s Ettore Bugatti, by now nicknamed 'the Patron' by his associates, devoted much of his energy to engineering and designing, the result of which was the most successful racer, an eight-cylinder Bugatti 35. Big-name drivers such as Chiron, Varzi, Dreyfus, and de Vizcaya contributed to almost 2000 Bugatti victories between 1924 and 1927.

However, even this success could not make Bugatti increase his volume of production. 'The Patron' invested all his profits in new, technically-advanced designs. Moreover, he became notorious for his thriftiness. He even saved on his best racing drivers. It is said that once he offered a chassis to Dreyfus instead of his wages.

Another car emerged in Molsheim in 1927, the Royale 41, the most luxurious, the most expensive, and the biggest car in the world. Only six or seven were built.

As time went by the responsibility for the works management devolved on Bugatti's son, Jean. Ettore Bugatti died in 1947 in an American hospital at Neuille. In 1951 the Molsheim works attempted a Bugatti come-back, with the 101 and 102 models, but without success.

CADILLAC

The beginnings of the Cadillac trademark date from 1899. In that year Henry Ford, backed by the mayor of the city of Detroit, established his first car works, the Detroit Automobile Company. It was not a financial success, and it passed into the hands of a millionaire named Murphy, who renamed it the Cadillac Automobile Co. This name was chosen in honour of the founder of Detroit, the French nobleman Antoine de la Mothe Cadillac.

The first single-cylinder A models were fitted with a horizontal engine and a two-speed epicyclic gearbox. More successful was the 1906 K model powered by a four-cylinder engine developing 22kW (30hp), with a top speed of 80km/h (50mph). By 1914 some 75,000 of this model had been sold.

In September 1908 the General Motors Company was established by William Crapo Durant, a millionaire from Flint, Mich., and an owner of the Buick car company. A month later he bought the Oldsmobile trademark, a year later the Oakland Co, the forerunner of Pontiac, and finally in 1909 the Cadillac Co, with Henry M. Leland as its manager.

Leland was a skilled toolmaker who had worked for the armament king Samuel Colt. Capitalizing on his experience of high quality production, he instituted a thorough technical inspection of work at all stages. This technical excellence was recognized by the British Royal Automobile Club, and the Cadillac trademark was awarded the Dewar Prize for exceptional achievements in the development of car engineering. In this particular case it was awarded for the complete interchangeability of all parts. A random selection of the K models from three different warehouses was carried out, all were taken apart and the parts were mixed and then re-assembled. The tests gave results identical to those obtained from the original cars.

Up to 1911 all car engines were started manually with a starting handle, which resulted in several accidents. In February 1911 Cadillac cars were fitted with the first Delco starters — and Cadillac was awarded its second Dewar Prize for this innovation.

In 1917 General Motors split with Henry Leland, who established a new company called the Lincoln Motor Co.

At that time Cadillac manufactured V8 engines only. In the 1930s its models were fitted with 12- or even 14-cylinder engines, thus bringing the Cadillac trademark to the very top of the American car market, not only in the number of cylinders, but also by its prices which were four times as much as those of an ordinary car.

CITRÖEN

The Citröen automobile company started making cars in Paris in 1919, with a gear wheel as its symbol. André Citröen was born in 1878, the fifth child of a Dutch diamond dealer. At the age of 23 he graduated from a technical college and established a works in Paris producing gearwheels. He obtained a licence from Russia for machining the V-shaped teeth, which guaranteed quiet running and a great load capacity. This works, in which Citröen was technical, commercial, and management director all in one, soon left all its competitors behind. The name of the young entrepreneur was widely recognized, and it won him the post of technical director with the Mors automobile company.

During the First World War Citröen proved his ability by erecting a factory for mass production of shells on the Quai de Javel in Paris. He also organized supplies of coal, natural gas, and provisions, and he introduced food rationing cards. Meanwhile he visited America twice, and at the Ford automobile company he made the acquaintance of American car manufacturing technology.

In 1919 Citröen and Jules Salemon, the designer of the popular Le Zébre, started manufacturing cars in the former ammunition works at the Quai de Javel. The first car was the A model, with a 1.3 litre engine devloping 7.4kW (10hp). The daily production of 100 vehicles was unbelievable when compared with the standards of the French car industry at that time. In four years the production increased to 300 cars a day. It was then that Citröen introduced a new 'people's car', the 5CV Tréfle model.

Citröen's name became famous also thanks to advertising. Pilots 'painted' his name in the sky, and in 1925, at the opening ceremony of an international exhibition in Paris, the name appeared in lights on the Eiffel tower. Citröen started his own car service, an insurance company, and blue and yellow traffic signs. The B2 model, developing 14.8kW (20hp), and fitted with a half-track chassis, was the first car to drive across the Sahara. The C4 model was driven across Central Asia and the arctic region of Canada. Citröen mailed gramophone records to his customers, advertising his cars.

The Great Depression of the 1930s led to 60 per cent of Citröen's shares being taken over by Michelin tyres. Citröen died in 1935: he did not live to see the success of the revolutionary model 7 with its front-wheel drive, which has been a feature of Citröen ever since.

DAIMLER

Gottlieb Daimler was born in 1834 in Schorndorf, some 30 km (19 mi) east of Stuttgart, the second of four children of a baker, Johannes Daimler. After finishing his mechanical engineering studies at Stuttgart Technical College he spent two years in England working for an engineering company. He and his friend Wilhelm Maybach settled at Bad Cannstatt in 1882. There in August 1883 he built the first high-speed gas engine, which was soon patented.

Three years later Daimler designed the first four-wheeler car. The chassis and the body were supplied by the royal carriage works, W. Wimpf & Son of Stuttgart. The first public trial run of Daimler's automobile took place on March 4, 1887.

In 1889 Daimler abandoned the carriage shape and designed a steel chassis for his car. This car, with steel wheels, he called the Stahlradwagen, and it was fitted with a V-twin engine. The car was exhibited with great success at the Paris World Exhibition.

Mercedes was the name of a new Daimler model, which took part in races from 1901. Although Wilhelm Maybach was its designer, the production was encouraged by Emil Jellinek, the Austro-Hungarian Consul-General in Nice and Daimler's distributor in France. After the victory of the Daimler Phoenix in the 1899 Nice-Castellane-Puget-Thermiers-Nice race, in which he had entered a car he called Mercédès after his 11-year-old daughter, Jellinek ordered 36 such cars for the French market. More victories followed, and from 1902 the name Mercedes was adopted for all Daimler cars.

Three weeks before the 1903 Gordon Bennett Trophy there was fire at the Cannstatt works. It destroyed much of the factory and its machinery, together with 60 newly-built cars, of which three had been prepared for the race. The cause of the fire remains a mystery. The factory was moved to Stuttgart-Untertürkheim, and Paul Daimler took over as director.

After the First World War there followed a period of financial success, thanks to the Mercedes Knight 16/50 PS, equipped with a sleeve-valve engine designed by Paul Daimler following the patent of the American, Charles Knight. In 1921 the company began to make supercharged engines. In June 1926 Daimler merged with Benz as Daimler-Benz AG.

DE DION-BOUTON

One day in 1882 an eccentric Paris aristocrat, Count Albert de Dion, discovered a small steam engine, a toy which captivated him entirely. He soon met its producers, Georges Bouton and M. Trépardoux, and offered them a financial share in a new company. Thus was born a new French car trademark, de Dion, Bouton & Trépardoux, originally producing tricycles and four-wheelers fitted with bicycle wheels and powered by steam engines.

At the Paris World Exhibition in 1889 de Dion saw Daimler's vehicles, and he registered a patent on his own combustion engine. This puny 0.37kW (0.5bhp) engine did not run at 180 rpm as Otto's did, nor at 450 rpm as that of Benz, but at the unbelievably high speed of 3000 rpm. However, the company continued supplying the market with powerful steam cars until it made its first petrol car in 1895.

In the 1890s a strong campaign was organized in Paris against the smelly and noisy petrol-driven cars. De Dion responded to it by a witty poster campaign. The poster depicted the kidnapping of a scantily-clothed beauty in a de Dion-Bouton car, which was getting away from pursuers on horses and motorcycles. Parisians showed their appreciation of its humour by buying more de Dion cars.

The company's popularity was also increased by the de Dion axle, which was patented in 1893, and first used in production in 1899. It was a rigid axle connecting both wheels, and this made them move in parallel. The driving force was transmitted by drive shafts terminating in propeller joints at both ends. A differential gear was fitted to a sprung section of the vehicle. The de Dion axle attempted to combine the advantages of a rigid axle and independently mounted wheels. It was not the cumbersome design but rather the breaking of the materials used that made this invention pass into oblivion, and the 1911 models were once again fitted with the traditional rigid axles.

The last car made by de Dion-Bouton was produced in 1952.

FIAT

On July 1, 1899, nine leading personalities of Piedmont, among them Giovanni Angelli, later president of the firm, founded a company called Societa Italiana per la construzione e il commercio delle automobili. Later this rather awkward name was changed to Fabbrica Italiana Automobili Torino, or FIAT for short. Its first car was built in the factory of Ceirano and Co which also became part of Fiat's property. It was a small vehicle developing 2.6kW (3.5hp), in which the passengers faced one another. Eight more cars were manufacturered in the same year. Notable was one with a twin-cylinder rear-mounted engine instead of the then common single-cylinder. The following year the 6, 8, 10 and 12 PS were among the new models.

Ford's introduction of mass production was copied by Fiat in Turin. At the Corso Dante factory a prototype of the new Fiat Zero was built. It was the first production car with this trademark. After the First World War Fiat took over several factories, including the Ferriere Piemontesi steel plant and Industrie Metallurgiche, Turin.

The greatest post-war success was the new Fiat 501 model, which was manufactured until 1926. Other cars offered were the four-cylinder 505 model, the 510 six-cylinder model, and the luxurious

Super Fiat fitted with a 6800 cc six-cylinder engine. The company built new works at Lingetto; the main assembly was based in two five-storey buildings, each 500m (1640ft) long, with a continuous manufacturing process moving from one floor to another. The roofs of both buildings served as trial tracks.

At the 1932 Milan exhibition the Fiat 508 Balilla was introduced. This model became to Fiat what the Model T had been to Ford. It had a 995 cc four-cylinder engine developing 14.7kW (20hp) and with a top speed of 80km/h (50mph). In no time Fiats had virtually flooded the world car market.

The company's present-day slogan, 'Fiat on land, sea, and air' indicates the scope of the Turin giant. It manufactures railcars, aircraft, helicopters, ship's engines, and turbines, and has a large investment programme.

FORD

In 1899, when the first Oldsmobile appeared on the roads, Henry Ford founded the Detroit Automobile Company. The cars were not in the luxury range, but were rather popular utility cars for farmers, who at that time represented 95 per cent of America's population. These people needed vehicles with good performance, simple maintenance, and a low price. To meet these objectives, the development of Ford's first cars demanded more time and money than the company's financial backers had anticipated. So the Detroit Automobile Company was sold, and this gave rise to Cadillac, a trademark later known for its luxurious models.

But Ford did not give up. Two racing victories in 1903 by his cars established their worth, and Ford soon raised the $100,000 he needed to establish his new Ford Motor Company. The first engines he used were supplied by Horace and John Dodge.

Another man coming on the automobile stage was a Rochester, N.Y. lawyer, George B. Selden, who had been carrying a patent on a 'road steamer' in his pocket ever since 1879. With this patent Selden attempted to create a monopoly, and coerce other manufacturers to become members of his 'trust' after paying an appropriate and far from modest admission fee. Ford responded by establishing the so-called Anti-Selden Syndicate. He hired the best lawyers and sent a team of experts to Europe to study all the patents on engines since 1879. Thus the designs of Siegfried Marcus were brought to light again. In 1911 a U.S. court of appeal annulled Selden's patent. Ford having won, concentrated all his efforts on the production of his ninth model, the multi-purpose Model T. This, Ford's most popular model, was in production for 19 years.

Despite the first signs of the Depression in 1929, technical advancement continued in Detroit. Ford spread his sales all over America. He avoided high export taxes in Europe by establishing factories in England and Germany. Today Ford is one of the world's largest car firms.

HISPANO-SUIZA

The Hispano-Suiza car company was founded in 1904, in Barcelona, under the name of La Hispano-Suiza Fábrica de Automobiles. Its forerunner was the Spanish firm Castro, which had been making cars since 1901. The young Swiss engineer Marc Birkigt was in from the beginning, and he was responsible for many successful designs under this trademark. The first models carried the original Castro emblem.

The Alfonso model was the most popular car of this period. It was named after the Spanish king, Alfonso XIII, who drove this automobile in a record drive from San Sebastian to Madrid.

From 1911 the Spanish cars were assembled at the new Societé Française Hispano-Suiza works in France. At first Marc Birkigt established a branch factory here, and later an independent company, Société Française Hispano-Suiza Bois Colombes-Seine. Apart from producing cars the works also manufactured outstanding aircraft engines, V8-ohc engines developing as much as 220kW (300bhp). The company's emblem, represented a flying stork, in honour of the echelon of Captain G. Guynemer, famous for an act of chivalry: in an air fight he spared E. Udet, a German pilot of a pursuit plane whose machine-gun broke down.

The 1919 Paris Salon brought a sensation, the H6 model. The engine design was inspired by an aircraft engine which had made the trademark famous: during the First World War more than 50,000 of these engines were produced for the French aircraft Spad, British SES, and American JN4H. The H6 was manufactured as a luxury tourer, and in a modified sports version it was supplied as the Monza and Boulogne models. The Monza became famous for its race with the American Stutz on the Indianapolis track. Over 24 hours the Monza maintained an average speed of 112km/h (70mph). The Boulogne broke eight records at Brooklands by covering 482 km (300 mi) at an average speed of 146km/h (90mph).

The Spanish division of Hispano-Suiza in Barcelona was involved in the production of powerful and attractive cars as late as 1944. The French branch at Bois Colombes near Paris ceased to exist in 1938.

HORCH

August Horch was among the first engineers who became famous for car designing. He was born in 1868, and at the age of 28 he was head of production at Benz & Co. in Mannheim. There he became familiar with volume car production.

After three years Horch left Benz and started designing his own vehicle in Cologne, working in a building which used to be a stable. A year later his first car was on the road. He established the firm of August Horch & Co, Motorwagenwerke AG, with its head office in Zwickau. The first car produced was the 18/22 PS model, fitted with an in-line four-cylinder engine.

The professional world was startled by Horch's numerous engineering novelties. He developed a noiseless gearbox with permanent mesh gears. He was the first person to use chrome-nickel steel for gear wheels. He inserted a clutch with a leather lining between the engine and the gearbox. The propeller shaft was mounted between the gearbox and the rear driving axle for the first time.

The company's victory with the 18/22 PS model in the 1906 Herkomer race not only brought fame to the firm, but also a fair number of orders. Unfortunately, the third Herkomer race was a failure, which caused skirmishes between Horch and the other shareholders. In June 1909 Horch left the firm and established a new company in Zwickau. His new car works was named Audi, the Latin translation of Horch's name. The original company concentrated on the production of luxurious and expensive cars.

A 1932 12-cylinder model was one of the stars of Horch's production programme. Its 600 V-engine developed 89kW (120hp) at 3000 rpm. It had a unique system of piston lubrication, and hydraulic control of valve clearance.

Also in 1932 Auto Union AG was founded, the emblem of which consisted of four interconnected circles symbolizing all car types produced by the concern — the puny DKW, medium-sized Wanderers, big Audis, and luxurious Horchs.

The company was nationalized in 1947 and re-named Sachsenring Kraftfahrzeug und Motorenwerk Zwickau/Sa. Horch's name vanished from the car scene in 1957.

ISOTTA-FRASCHINI

Cesare Isotta and the Fraschini brothers, Vincenzo, Oreste, and Antonio, founded the Societé Milanese d'Automobili Isotta-Fraschini in 1899 in Milan. At first they manufactured the French Renault and Mors under licence, but two years later they started building their own cars. Of great significance to the firm was the arrival of a promising engineer, Giustino Cattaneo. He had considerable skill in designing successful racing cars. One of these cars won the 1908 Targa Florio circuit. In 1910 Cattaneo had his front braking axle patented, and the Isotta-Fraschini firm was the first in the world to fit its cars with brakes on all four wheels.

Drawing from experience gained in building aircraft engines during the First World War, Isotta Fraschini introduced its first big automobile, the Tipo 8, in 1919. It was fitted with a 5902 cc eight-cylinder engine. From then on Isotta-Fraschini was regarded as a symbol of the best quality in cars during the 1920s. The firm established agencies in America, Argentina, Brazil, Britain, France, Spain, Belgium, and Switzerland.

By the end of 1924 the 8A model was fitted with a bigger engine of 7300 cc, which developed 81-89kW (110-120hp) — Isotta-Fraschini never specified exactly the power of their engines. After the synchromesh gearbox was introduced by Cadillac in 1929, Isotta-Fraschini fitted its Tipo 8B with the Wilson preselector four-speed gearbox.

In 1935 the firm got into financial difficulties. Its last attempt at a comeback was at the 1947 Paris show, where the firm exhibited an interesting prototype 8C Monterosa with a rear V8-engine. Only four of these cars were made, and in February 1948 the Isotta-Fraschini factory gates closed for the last time.

JAGUAR

In 1922 two young motorcycle enthusiasts, William Lyons and William Walmsley, set up a company in Blackpool called the Swallow Sidecar Company, with an initial capital of £1000. The company, as its name indicates, produced sidecars for motorcycles.

In 1926 circumstances favoured the production of automobile bodywork. And so, there appeared the small Austin Seven, a 'people's car' of rather Spartan design. The company changed its name to the Swallow Sidecar and Coachbuilding Co.

The limited space in Blackpool made the company look for a bigger manufacturing area in Coventry. There it made bodies for such cars as Morris Cowley, Fiat 509, Wolseley Hornet, and Standard.

The company's first car, the SS, was based on a six-cylinder engine produced by Standard. It was introduced to the public at a London exhibition in 1931. The SS was a long, low vehicle with a short passenger compartment and a luggage boot with a spare tyre at the rear. These features were used by other acknowledged coachbuilders, such as Figoni and Van Vooren.

The firm's production programme included limousines, convertibles, and sports cars fitted with 1.5-, 2.5-, and 3.5-litre engines. The most notable vehicle of the period was the 3.5-litre SS 100 model, the fastest and most famous pre-war Jaguar.

Production after the Second World War resumed in 1946, when the company's name was changed to Jaguar Cars Ltd. William Lyons had encouraged the updating of older models, and he developed a new sports car, the XK 120, fitted with a six-cylinder × 2 OHC engine with a capacity of 3442 cc. The vehicle, with pressed aluminium bodywork, was inspired by the successful BMW 328 model. In the Le Mans Rally a modified version was used, the XK 120 C, with a six-cylinder engine developing 185kW (250hp), which began a series of victories in 1951, 1953, 1955, 1956, and 1957.

In 1960 Daimler, with its share in the BSA factory, was bought by Jaguar Cars Ltd. Eight years later the largest British motor car complex had been established by merging with Leyland.

LANCIA

In 1906 Vincenzo Lancia, test and racing driver of Fiat, and his friend, the notary public Claudio Fogolini, established a small motor company in Turin, Fabbrica di Automobili, Lancia et Co.

From the very beginning the company concentrated on producing light sports cars fitted with powerful engines. The first model was the Lancia Alfa, which was announced in 1908. This was followed by other models with 'classical' names such as Kappa and Trikappa. In 1922 the company introduced a new, unconventional Lambda model. In 1924 the following comment appeared in the German car magazine

Allgemeine Automobil Zeitung: 'The Lancia Lambda is of such a unique design that it can be referred to as a revolutionary phenomenon in automotive engineering'. What brought the car this accolade were independent front wheel suspension, narrow compact V4-engine with the camshaft in the cylinder head, and a light integral body.

Vincenzo Lancia always strove to produce high quality cars, even at the cost of using more expensive engineering designs. Examples include the hydraulic brakes of the Augusta in 1932; rear axle torsion bar suspension and an aerodynamic body shell for the 1937 Aprilia model; the de Dion rear axle of the Aurelia in 1953; and the front wheel drive and engine with opposed pistons of the 1961 Flavia model.

Although Vincenzo Lancia had raced Fiat cars until 1908 and won many cups, he was not interested in a racing programme for his own cars. The company, however, changed its view in the 1950s. In 1954 Louis Chiron won the Monte Carlo Rally and Alberto Ascari won the Mille Miglia. The Lancia D 50 racer, fitted with a V8-engine, and racing under Ferrari colours, became the most successful formula car of 1956 when Juan Manuel Fangio won his fourth world championship.

In the 1930s Lancia had started producing luxurious cars for the wealthy. Astura, Augusta, and Artena were among the notable models. In 1960, after producing the luxury limousine Flaminia styled by Pininfarina, the firm founded the most elite club in the world. Its membership was limited to people who bought at least six new Lancias within a certain time limit. Each member was given two badges, one for the car and another to be worn on a jacket. The badge colour indicated the number of cars purchased.

Ever-growing competition from other car manufacturers finally made Lancia merge with the financially more powerful Fiat.

PANHARD & LEVASSOR

In 1891 Panhard & Levassor was the first company to produce a French automobile. Several people and events were behind this firm. Gottlieb Daimler, the German engine manufacturer, had an agent in Paris, Eduard Sarazin. He and Daimler were friends for many years. Before his death Sarazin handed over his business affairs to his wife, Louise. They included a contractual arrangement for Panhard & Levassor, originally makers of woodworking machinery, to build Daimler engines.

Louise Sarazin was eager to carry on her husband's business, and therefore she visited Daimler at Cannstatt to find out his future plans. As a result of this meeting a new contract was concluded giving the exclusive representation of Daimler in France to Mme. Sarazin.

In 1889 Daimler sent his Stahlradwagen to the Paris World Exhibition, which coincided with the 100th anniversary of the French revolution. The car was a sensation, and French companies tried hard to obtain patents and licences on its production. It was Mme. Sarazin who succeeded, and with the patents in her pocket she married René Levassor and offered all rights to Panhard & Levassor. After the Paris Exhibition was over, Emil Levassor and René Panhard started producing automobiles of their own design fitted with Daimler engines. A year and a half later, in May 1891, they completed their first production car.

Levassor realized that lasting commercial success depended on success on the racetrack, and he took part personally in events in his own cars. He was unlucky in the 1896 Paris-Marseille-Paris race in which he led, to be involved in a bad crash, dying of his injuries the following year. This race was won by a colleague in a Panhard & Levassor car.

Levassor spared no pains to perfect the design of his cars. He originated the concept of the front-mounted engine, and a gearbox with sliding gear wheels, and designed a new friction clutch and a radiator. In 1898 Levassor introduced the steering wheel, and he was the first to use aluminium in engine production. It was largely due to him that the automobile ceased to look like a carriage. He regarded motor-racing as the best test of a car's engineering properties.

34

His partner and friend, the modest René Panhard, died in the middle of 1908. At that time the company was a leader in French motor racing, and scoring one victory after the other. During the first decade of motor racing the company won 12 international events. In 1908 the firm was among the few European companies which obtained a licence from the American Knight company to make a sleeve-valve engine.

Panhard & Levassor, the oldest French automobile trademark, existed until 1965, when it merged with the more powerful Citröen.

PEUGEOT

In 1810 the Peugeot brothers, Jean Frederick and Jean Pierre, set up a small metal foundry at Sous-Cretet which became the basis of a family enterprise. In 1885 the third Peugeot generation, the brothers Eugène and Armand, started thinking about changing the firm, then making bicycles and tricycles, over to car production.

Armand Peugeot realized that the then popular steam-engine had no future, and he turned to petrol-driven engines. In 1888 he concluded an arrangement with Panhard & Levassor for a supply of Daimler engines, produced under licence, and two years later the first Peugeot car left the factory. It had *Vis-à-Vis* seating and was powered by a twin-cylinder Daimler engine. The car was fitted with a gearbox, and had a top speed of 25km/h (15mph). In the Paris-Brest-Paris cycle race it was used as an accompanying car, and covered the 2057 km (1278 mi) long course at an average speed of 14.7km/h (9.25mph).

35

Peugeot's biggest success came in the most important event of 1894, the Paris-Rouen race, in which five Peugeot cars finished, fulfilling the conditions for the most successful automobile.

The first prize of 5000 gold francs, given by *Le Petit Journal*, was shared by Peugeot and Levassor.

In 1895 the first world motor race was held, the Paris-Bordeaux-Paris race. Twenty-one cars started on the demanding 1200 km (746 m) long course, among them Panhard & Levassor, de Dion, Benz, Bollée, and Peugeot. Levassor was disqualified, and Koechlin won the race driving a Peugeot. L'Eclaire was another specially-designed car of Peugeot make which took part in the race. It was fitted with Michelin tyres, which were among the latest novelties of the motoring world. Michelin himself drove the car and repaired the tyres when they went flat.

Success in motor racing led to increased orders for Peugeot cars. In 1896 Armand Peugeot established an independent car company at Audincourt, called Societé des Automobile Peugeot. Racers remained a priority in the events and rallies organized during the pre-war period, and all new ideas tried in the races were fitted to the production cars. In 1914 Peugeot cars were fitted with brakes on all four wheels.

The wide range of production cars included the light Bébé, designed by Ettore Bugatti; the Quadrillette, built in 1920 with electric self-starting and lighting; and the 1921 Cyclecar, weighing 345kg (761lb).

The company prospered thanks to excellent craftsmanship, and attractive styling which was the work of the Pininfarina coachbuilding company.

RENAULT

At the turn of the century quite a number of engineers turned to designing cars. A small workshop or a smithy furnished with a lathe was almost as much as they needed for assembling a vehicle. But only a few automobile pioneers managed to implement their plans on a large scale. One of the fortunate ones was Louis Renault.

As early as 1898 he built his first automobile, fitted with a de Dion engine, in a small workshop at the far end of his garden. A year later this garden shed enterprise had become a company owned by the Renault brothers. The company's emblem consisted of the symmetrically intertwined initial letters L (for Louis), M (Marcel), F (Fernand), and R (Renault).

In 1900 the company won a series of events. First was the Paris-Toulouse-Paris race followed by Paris-Berlin, Paris-Vienna, ending up with the tragic 1903 Paris-Madrid circuit. In this event Marcel Renault was fatally injured, and the responsibility for the company was taken over by Louis Renault.

The pioneer deeds of the company include the first closed limousine, the first taxi-cab, and the first bus with 21 seats.

In 1909, after Fernand's death, Louis established a shareholding company of Renault factories called Société Anonyme des Usines Renault.

Ever-increasing production called for more precise planning and systematic development. Renault had enlarged his design department as well as the whole company; he hired new workers and in the early 1920s his was amongst the biggest European car companies. In 1925 the bonnets of his cars were fitted with the well-known diamond-styled trademark, which originally covered the horn.

Apart from private cars, Renault made commercial vehicles and tractors, and he supplied engines for ships, aircraft, and industry. A year after Louis Renault's death in 1944 the company was nationalized and the name changed to Régie Nationale des Usines Renault. In 1947 some 27,000 of the 4 CV model left the assembly lines, and Renaults captured records in such races as the Monte Carlo Rally, Le Mans 24 Hours, Mille Miglia and Alpine Rally. In 1954 the 500,000th Renault 4 CV left the assembly line.

The managing director, Pierre Lefaucheux, an engineer and doctor of law, continued the line of the dynamic advancement and development into the present-day industrial giant.

ROLLS-ROYCE

Frederick Henry Royce was born in 1863 in Alwalton, Huntingdonshire, and began his career as an electrician. At the age of 21 he began making dynamos and electrical appliances. But in 1903 his business, F. H. Royce and Co, went bankrupt because of the cheaper products of his German and American competitors. After this Royce set his mind on perfecting an old Décauville car, and the outcome of his efforts was to turn this vehicle into a completely new car. Royce's first cars appeared in 1904. They were fitted with twin-cylinder engines, about which *The Times* made the following comment. 'The passenger does not hear nor feel when the engine is running'.

The company's reputation increased after the Hon. Charles Stewart joined the firm. Rolls, the third son of Lord Llangattock, was born in 1877. He and his partner Claude Johnson owned a company importing cars. After a meeting in Manchester both companies agreed to produce and sell cars under the trademark Rolls-Royce.

The first Rolls-Royce was fitted with a 1.8 litre twin-cylinder engine developing 7.4kW (10hp). This model was followed by cars powered by three-, four- or six-cylinder engines. The 1906 six-cylinder model 40/50 HP proved so successful that Johnson, now a director of the company, decided to discontinue production of all others. The quietly running six-cylinder engine, the silver-plated parts, and the silver-varnished aluminium body of the 40/50 HP model were among the car's assets, giving the name of 'Silver Ghost' to the 13th car manufactured in this series. From 1913 these cars were identified by the famous radiator mascot of the Spirit of Ecstasy, commonly called 'Emily'.

The firm had never shown much taste for revolutionary technological advances and its coachwork, though modified every 10 years, always gave an impression of solidness. This was due to such leading coachbuilders as Park Ward-Mulliner, Barker and James Young.

Charles Rolls, a sports enthusiast, became in 1910 the first person to make a double crossing of the English Channel, but he was killed in an air crash a few months later. Sir Henry Royce, one of the best designers in the motoring industry, was made a baronet in 1930, and died in 1933. After his death the original red R R letters on the radiator were changed to black. What remained unchanged was the reliability of the company's products capitalizing on thorough inspection and choice of quality materials right from the very beginning. Each part has its file card containing all necessary data, test results, and the names of operators and quality inspection personnel. All engines are tested under full load for seven hours, and then each engine is taken to pieces and checked. Rolls-Royce inspectors test to destruction every 20th chassis. 14 different coatings protect the car's body against corrosion.

The company's slogan is 'Perfection'. Therefore personalities such as Queen Elizabeth, the Queen of the Netherlands, many other European heads of state, Indian maharajahs, Arab oil sheiks, and African potentates are to be found among the firm's clients. In short, it is a company that needs no advertising department.

TATRA

In 1897 car production was started in part of the former Austro-Hungarian empire that is now Czechoslovakia. The year before, through a textile works owner, Theodor von Liebig of Reichenberg (present-day Liberec), the Kopřivnice motor company, Nesselsdorfer Wagenbaufabrik in Moravia, purchased Benz's single-cylinder motor car and a twin-cylinder engine. The company then announced its 'President' model. The firm used its own 'Mylord' carriage design, which had sold well, and fitted to it a 2.75 litre horizontally-opposed twin-cylinder Benz engine developing 5.2kW (7hp) at 600 rpm. In 1898 the President covered the distance between Kopřivnice and Vienna at an average speed of 22.6km/h (14mph). In Vienna it was introduced to the public. This car started the era of Kopřivnice car production. It was followed by the Vicepresident, Wien, Meteor, Aufhof, Spitzbub, and other models.

The cars also made their mark in international racing. Baron Liebig won the 1899 race in Vienna and a year later he won the hill climb in Nice.

In 1914 the company's cars were fitted with brakes on all four wheels, which was rather unusual at that time.

After the First World War the U models, fitted with a 48.1kW (65hp) engine and brakes on all wheels, were tested in the High Tatra. After obtaining excellent results in this mountainous terrain the Kopřivnice Nesselsdorfer Wagenbaufabrik trademark was changed to Tatra. A new factory was built which produced the renowned Tatra II model, fitted with a central frame, rear swing axles and an air-cooled engine developing 9kW (12hp). This design was characteristic of Tatras as late as 1934, when the last car of this model was produced.

In the 1930s Tatra became known for its streamlined 77 model, fitted with an air-cooled eight-cylinder engine. By mounting the engine at the rear Tatra started an era continued by the 87 and 97 models, remaining unchanged even after 1945 when the company was nationalized.

THE CAR IN HISTORY

1490 Leonardo da Vinci built a hand-propelled vehicle.

1545 The Italian mathematician Geronimo Cardano invented the universal joint.

1673 The Dutch physicist Christiaan Huygens constructed an atmospheric piston engine.

1769 The Scottish mechanic James Watt patented a steam engine with a separate condenser.
The French military engineer Nicolas Joseph Cugnot built a steam three-wheeler.

1801 The English mining engineer Richard Trevithick built a steam carriage, 'Captain Dick's Puffer', the direct predecessor of the locomotive.

1806 A Swiss, Major Isaac de Rivaz, constructed a self-propelling vehicle with an internal-combustion engine and electric ignition.

1841 An English mechanic, Joseph Whitworth, developed a unified thread system.

1844 The American chemist, Charles Goodyear, invented vulcanization of raw rubber.

1845 AN Edinburgh shop assistant, Robert William Thomson, invented the pneumatic tyre and had it patented.

1859 A French physicist, Gaston Planté, invented the lead accumulator.

1860 A French waiter, Jean-Joseph Étienne Lenoir, built a gas engine with electric ignition.

1866 The German electrical engineer, Werner Siemens, developed a self-exciting electric dynamo.

1875 The Viennese designer, Siegfried Marcus, built an automobile fitted with a petrol engine and a low-tension magneto ignition.

1876   A Cologne shop assistant, Nikolaus August Otto, was granted a patent on a four-stroke gas engine.

1885   Karl Benz built a three-wheeled motor car.
Gottlieb Daimler constructed the Petroleum Reitwagen, the first motorcycle in the world.

1886   Daimler introduced his first four-wheeler.

1887   Benz developed the first electric ignition for low-revving engines.

1888   The Scottish veterinary surgeon, John Boyd Dunlop, was granted a patent on the bicycle tyre.

1893   The German engineer, Wilhelm Maybach, and the Hungarian inventor, Donát Bánki, independently developed a jet carburettor.

1895   The first car races took place in Europe (Paris-Bordeaux-Paris) and in America (Chicago-Waukegan-Chicago).
The French Automobile Club was established.

1896   F. W. Lanchester built the first British motor vehicle.
The Frenchman, Édouard Michelin, used removable tyres.

1898   The first car exhibition was held at the Tuilleries in Paris.

1899   The 100km/h (62mph) speed was exceeded for the first time by the Belgian Camille Jenatzy driving a 'Jamais Contente' car.

1900   The first Mercedes prototype was designed, having the characteristic features of a modern vehicle.

1901   G. Hanold developed a high-tension magneto for the high-revving engines.

1902   Louis Renault was granted a patent on a radial engine supercharger.

1903   The American bicycle engineers, Wilbur and Orville Wright, flew the first engine-powered airplane.

1904   The first ladies' automobile club was established.

1905   End of the Antique cars era.

1906   First French Grand Prix.

1907   Long-distance trial, Peking-Paris.

1908   General Motors Corporation was established.

1910   Britain introduced motor vehicle taxation.
First production cars with brakes on all four wheels were introduced.

1911   The first car with an electric starter (Cadillac) was built.

1916   American car production topped 1,000,000 a year.

1918 End of the Veteran cars era.
1919 Beginning of the Vintage cars era.
1921 American cars were fitted with hydraulic brakes.
1922 Introduction of balloon tyres.
1923 Brakes fitted at all four wheels were common practice.
1926 The Daimler and Benz companies merged as Daimler-Benz AG.
1927 Introduction of petrol octane numbers.
      First car radio used in America.
1929 'Black Friday' on the New York Stock Exchange and the beginning of the Depression.
1930 The Classic cars era began.
1931 The first front-wheel-drive two-stroke car (DKW) was built.
1932 Low-pressure tyres ousted the balloon tyres.
1933 Aerodynamic principles were applied for the first time to mass produced cars.
1935 Sir Malcolm Campbell set a world speed record of 485.175km/h (301.48mph) on the Great Salt Lake.
1936 The first Mercedes car with a diesel engine was made.
1938 The foundation stone of the Volkswagen factory was laid.
1939 Every second American family had a car.
1940 End of the Classic cars era.

THE MAKES

An illustrated account follows, describing international achievement in the manufacture of some of the world's finest cars made between 1770 and 1940.

CUGNOT   1770

Manufactured by N. J. Cugnot, Paris, France

Nicolas Joseph Cugnot was born in Lorraine in 1725. In his early childhood he showed his knack for inventing. But since he lacked the necessary financial support to cover his experiments, he adopted a military career, and as a captain in the French army he produced many inventions, some of which are still in use. The steam engine stirred Cugnot's lively mind. He pondered over its application to a vehicle, but first of all he planned to cut down on its size and weight and increase its capacity.

In 1764 the French Minister of War entrusted him officially with building a steram tractor for carrying guns. Cugnot designed a model of a small artillery carriage, and in 1769 he demonstrated it near Ste Magdalene's church in Paris. The carriage had a speed of 4.5km/h (2¾mph), and one boiler filling lasted for a mere 12 minutes. The boiler had to be refilled and heated by a fire until it started generating steam, and only then could the next 12-minute run take place. Despite all these setbacks the steamer captivated the minister, and he immediately ordered Cugnot to make a bigger 'steamer'.

Cugnot presented this new vehicle to the military authorities on April 22, 1770. Its maximum speed was 4km/h (2½mph), but this time the vehicle was fitted with an internal furnace so that the boiler did not need to be heated from the ground. The twin-cylinder single-acting engine was mounted above the front wheel. The bronze cylinders had a bore and stroke of 325 × 378mm. The drive was transmitted from the piston rod to the wheel by a ratchet and pawl. Reverse could be engaged by tilting the pawl over.

During the demonstration, which started smoothly, the controls jammed and the vehicle hit a wall which collapsed. Despite this impact the vehicle did not suffer any damage, and it acquitted itself as a perfect artillery vehicle. But Cugnot's luck ran out when the minister fell into disgrace with the royal court. Cugnot, disappointed and forgotten by everybody, died in 1804 in Brussels.

But the furnace was lit once more to set the vehicle going, this time from the armoury to the Conservatoire National des Arts et Métiers in Paris, where it can be admired today.

MARCUS   1875

Manufactured by Lichtenstein Machinery Works, Adamov,
Austria-Hungary (now Blansko, Czechoslovakia)

Siegfried Marcus was born in 1831 at Malchinev, in Mecklenburg,
Germany. He worked as a mechanic with Siemens and Halke in Berlin.
In 1852 he moved to Vienna where he worked for a time at the
University of Vienna. After establishing his position in 1860, he could
devote his time to hobbies, among which electrical engineering
predominated.

He solved many problems, some of which were patented. In Austria-
Hungary alone he was granted 38 patents. His magneto-electric
ignition of 1864 was widely applied in internal-combustion engines.
The Marcus carburettor, patented in 1865, was applied in the Langen
& Wolf atmospheric engine, and later on in his own engine.

Since atmospheric engines were outmoded, Marcus concentrated
on Otto's four-stroke engines, based on compression. His newly
evolved combustion engine was manufactured by Jacob
Warchalowski of Vienna and Marky, Bromovský & Schulz of Prague,
who rented the Liechtenstein machinery works at Adamov, for this
purpose for the next 25 years.

Based on Marcus' designs, the horizontally-mounted four-stroke
single-cylinder was fitted into a car. Thus one of the very first self-
propelled automobiles was built. The car's chassis consisted of a
wooden frame with two benches. When steering, the front steel axle
turned round the vertical axis of the steering column. It was supported
on semi-elliptic springs. The rigid axle was mounted in two bearings
and carried on rubber joints. The steel-tyred rear wheels were
controlled by a block brake.

The single-cylinder engine, with a capacity of 570 cc, developed
0.73kW (1hp) at 300 rpm. The engine revolutions were adjusted by a
control valve. The carburettor was heated from a by-pass of the
exhaust pipe. The engine was cooled by water circulating from a tank
located beneath the rear seat. Friction clutches served as a differential,
and they were mounted directly in the wheel hubs.

The vehicle was made in the Liechtenstein machinery works at
Adamov near Brno. In 1898 the car was purchased by the Austrian
Motor Club, and is now exhibited in the Technical Museum in Vienna.

BENZ Patent-Motorwagen   1885/86

Manufactured by Benz & Co, Rheinische Gasmotoren-Fabrik,
Mannheim, Germany

In 1883 a new name appeared in Mannheim commercial circles. This
new enterprise was Benz & Co., Rheinische Gasmotoren-Fabrik. The
leading partner of the firm, Karl Benz, embarked on building a road
runner powered by a gas engine. Benz, being a cycle enthusiast, used
the frame of a tricycle as the most suitable chassis, with wire-spoked
wheels, and solid rubber tyres. The stationary twin-cylinder engine
built at his works had a range of 120-180 rpm, which could not set in
motion any carriage. Therefore Benz built a four-stroke single-cylinder
engine, developing 0.66kW (0.9hp) at 450 rpm. This 950 cc engine
was fitted with mechanically operated inlet valves instead of a slide
valve, electric ignition and water cooling. It had a huge horizontal
flywheel, which was mounted between the rear wheels. There was
only one small, easily operated wheel at the front for steering. The
drive transmission was like that of a bicycle, through belts and chains.
The vehicle weighed 263kg (580lb) and had a top speed of 12km/h
(7½mph). This, the first automobile in the world and nicknamed
'Benzine', was driven by Benz in the autumn of 1885. On January 29,
1886 Benz & Co. was granted a patent on a gas-powered vehicle.

Benz's cars became better known in France than in Germany thanks
to Emil Roger, Benz's Paris agent for distributing the twin-cylinder
stationary engines. Benz's wife, Bertha, and their sons, Eugen and
Richard, were the first to recognize the importance of popularizing
Benz's Patent-Motorwagen in Germany. Early one morning the boys
pushed 'Benzine' out of the garage without waking their father. They
started the engine up, the drove the car for 90 km (56 mi) to Pforzheim
to their grandmother's. The vehicle was driven by the 15-year-old
Eugen, with his mother seated beside him, and Richard at the back. In
the evening Karl Benz received a telegram: 'Arrived in Pforzheim
without any problems'.

The Patent-Motorwagen was awarded the gold medal at the 1888
Munich Exhibition of Industrial Goods. Benz drove his vehicle as owner
of the world's first driving licence, issued by the Baden authorities on
August 1, 1888.

Not more than 15 vehicles were produced in the period 1888-1893.
The original of the first Patent-Motorwagen can be seen in the Daimler-
Benz Museum in Stuttgart-Untertürkheim.

PANHARD & LEVASSOR   1891

Manufactured by Societé Anonyme des Anciens Establissements
Panhard & Levassor, Paris, France

The development of motoring in France is closely linked with Panhard & Levassor. René Panhard and Émile Levassor were engineers, and they took over a factory producing woodworking machinery. After obtaining a licence to make Daimler engines in 1890, they started car production.

From the very beginning Levassor strove to design a vehicle which would not resemble a carriage, and all parts of which would be designed especially to fit the automobile's purpose and function. He experimented with mounting the engine at the rear and in the middle, and finally he resolved the problem by fitting the horizontally opposed twin-cylinder at the front. It should be noted that this happened shortly after Levassor had said to his friend Peugeot: 'The engine should be at the rear so that the noise and fumes will be of the least irritation to the passengers'. Thus the 1891 Panhard & Levassor model became the first car with a front-mounted engine. It was a Daimler V-twin engine in which the cylinders formed a 20° angle and the connecting rods, with a delay of one revolution in ignition, operated the common crankshaft. The 1235 cc engine developed 1.84kW (2.5hp). Ignition was by a glow plug. The drive was transmitted from the engine through a clutch to a three-speed gearbox and further to the rear axle by a chain drive. The car's maximum speed was 30km/h (19mph). The reliability of this model is proved by a specimen which has been preserved. In the care of Abbot Gavois it had travelled 140,000 km (87,000 mi) by 1932.

Émile Levassor took part in motor racing, thus testifying to the advanced designs of his cars. In 1895 he won the non-stop 48-hour Paris-Bordeaux-Paris race. A year later he was the favourite in the biggest French Paris-Marseille-Paris event which was 1175 km (730 mi) long. Only an unfortunate accident made him lose the race. However, there was a sweeping one-two-three finish for Panhard & Levassor cars.

Levassor died in 1897 of an injury sustained in an accident, becoming the first victim of motor racing.

BENZ VICTORIA 1893

Manufactured by Benz & Co, Rheinische Gasmotoren-Fabrik,
Mannheim, Germany

One of the reasons for the poor commercial success of Benz's first
vehicle was that it was a tricycle. So from 1891 Benz embarked on
solving the front wheel steering problem. Two years later he did so by
swivelling the wheels independently on king pins, and he was granted
a patent. The new car was called Victoria, symbolizing victory over the
steering problem. The vehicle's excellent properties were tested not
only in city traffic but also on longer distances.

In 1894, the year Count Albert de Dion organized the very first Paris-
Rouen car race, a textile industrialist, Baron Theodor Liebig entered for
a long-distance race in Liberec, now in Czechoslovakia, at the wheel of
his Victoria. He and his friend Stransky chose the route from Liberec
via Mannheim to Rheims and back. On the first day they reached the
small town of Waldheim, having averaged 13.5km/h (8.4mph). The
town was some 195 km (121 mi) from Liberec, and the car reached a
top speed of 22km/h (14mph). The next stop-over was at Eisenberg
and Eisenach. The fourth day was the most strenuous, a non-stop
drive to Mannheim, the Victoria's home town. The drive took 26 hours.
Karl Benz personally welcomed the intrepid Baron Liebig and organized
a ball in his honour. The following day the drive continued to Gondorf
with a longer stop-over. By now the automobile had covered 1000 km
(620 mi). The pace from Condorf to Rheims and back to Liberec was
less hectic. Liebig recorded his experience in a diary, ending up with
the following: 'One of the things we appreciate highly is that Benz's
car has made us aware of all the beautiful places that exist in the
German countryside'.

The Benz Victoria, in which Baron Liebig covered the 2500 km
(1550 mi) route, was fitted with a horizontal single-cylinder engine.
With bore and stroke dimensions of 130×150mm it had a capacity of
2000 cc and developed 3kW (4hp) at 400 rpm. This four-stroke
water-cooled engine was mounted at the rear, and it drove the rear axle
by means of flat belts and two chains. The hand-brake controlled the
back wheels, which were fitted with solid rubber tyres. The vehicle
weighed 650kg (143lb) and it was 2.9m (9ft 6in) long.

The Victoria was Benz's favourite car. It was made in different
versions, such as Vis-à-vis or Phaeton, until 1899.

DAIMLER VIS-À-VIS   1894

Manufactured by Daimler-Motorengesselschaft, Cannstatt, Germany

After Daimler and Maybach's success with the Stahlradwagen, exhibited by Panhard & Levassor at the Paris World Show in 1899, another person who became interested in the 'Daimler system' vehicle was Armand Peugeot, who made bicycles and steam road-carriages. A close co-operation was established between Daimler and the French industrialists, and the foundations of the French motor car industry were laid.

The French press also encouraged the development of the French motor car industry. The year 1893 was not particularly lucky for French newspaper owners. Pierre Giffard, editor-in-chief of *Le Petit Journal*, realized that he would not win subscribers if there was no sensational material in his newspaper. Therefore he invited entries in *Le Petit Journal* for a race 'of all vehicles powered by steam, gas, petrol, or electricity'. The course was from Paris to Rouen. 14 petrol-powered and 7 steam-powered vehicles started the race on July 22, 1894. Among the vehicles were Panhard & Levassor, Roger-Benz, Peugeot, and de Dion. After 4 hours and 40 minutes Count Albert de Dion was the first to reach the finishing line in Rouen with his 14.7kW (20hp) steam vehicle. He was followed by two 3kW (4hp) Peugeots. Fourth was the Panhard & Levassor, driven by Émil Levassor. Considering the competition rules, it required more than just imagination to think of de Dion's heavy 'steam tractor' as a family vehicle. Therefore the jury decided that the first prize should be shared equally between Peugeot and Panhard & Levassor. Giffard, who awarded the prizes, made the following comment: 'Gottlieb Daimler and his engine, which powered Peugeot's and Panhard & Levassor's vehicles, deserve special approbation, for this engine has proved to be the best.'

In the same year Daimler, who had himself taken part in the race, designed a four-seater on the Vis-à-Vis pattern. This vehicle was fitted with a 1040 cc twin-cylinder four-stroke water-cooled engine. It developed 2.7kW (3.7hp) at 650 rpm. The drive was transmitted through a system of belts. The vehicle had a four-speed gearbox and solid rubber tyres, and it had a top speed of 22km/h (14mph). The original chassis is now displayed in the Daimler-Benz museum in Stuttgart-Untertürkheim.

RENAULT VOITURETTE   1898

Manufactured by Louis Renault, Billancourt, France

Louis Renault, the fourth son of his parents, built his first car in the family garden shed at Billancourt in 1898. he was 21 when he modified a de Dion tricycle to a four-wheeler Voiturette. Renault replaced the then common belts and noisy chains by a newly developed three-speed-and-reverse gearbox. The drive was transmitted via a propeller shaft to a differential at the rear axle. This system also became widely used in other cars, and in only slightly modified form it is still used on modern cars. Renault's first car was fitted with a single-cylindor water-cooled engine made by de Dion-Bouton, with bore and stroke of 66×80mm and of 273 cc. This front-mounted engine developed 1.3kW (1.75hp). The Voiturette weighed as little as 350kg (770lb) and with two passengers it had a top speed of 32km/h (20mph).

After showing the vehicle to his friends, Louis Renault received 12 orders for this car, the majority paid in advance. However, in order to make them, he had to build a bigger factory. And so, in partnership with his brothers Marcel and Fernand, the Société Renault Frères was established in 1899. In that year Renault produced 72 closed limousines, the Renault Coupé model, which was a novelty. In 1900 another model by the Renault brothers appeared, fitted with a more powerful 2.6kW (3.5hp) engine. The engines were supplied by de Dion-Bouton.

Two years later Renault Frères started making their own engines. The designer of these new twin-cylinder and four-cylinder water-cooled engines had worked in the de Dion-Bouton design department. Renault cars of this period were notable for their twin radiators, fitted alongside the bonnet. The radiators were easily accessible and at the same time well protected against dust.

The garden shed in which the history of Renault started still exists, and now it overlooks the Renault management offices in Emile Zola Avenue at Billancourt near Paris.

CANNSTATT DAIMLER   1898

Manufactured by Daimler-Motorengesellschaft, Cannstatt, Germany

The first engines and vehicles produced by Daimler at Cannstatt were more popular abroad than in Germany. The first Daimler in America was sold in 1893. In Britain the development of motoring was hampered by the 'Red Flag' Act, which set a speed limit of 6.4km/h (4mph), and said every vehicle must be preceded by a man on foot carrying a red flag. In 1896, when the 'Road-Steamer' Act legalized motoring in Britain, the financier Harry Lawson bought patents from Daimler and established the British Daimler Motor Company at Radford in Coventry. A drive by the Prince of Wales (the future King Edward VII) in a Daimler at Southampton was an official acknowledgement of Daimler cars. From then onwards Daimlers were traditionally used by the British Royal Family. Queen Elizabeth II broke this tradition, and started using a Rolls-Royce.

After the establishment of the Daimler Co. in Coventry, German Daimlers were distinguished as 'Cannstatt Daimlers' as opposed to the British models, called 'Coventry Daimlers'.

The German car shown here was fitted with a twin-cylinder engine cast in a single block for the first time. With bore and stroke dimensions of 100×140mm, the engine's capacity was 2200 cc. The exhaust valves were operated by a camshaft. The drive was transmitted to the rear axle via a four-speed gearbox. The engine developed 5.9kW (8hp), with a top speed of 40km/h (25mph).

A few years before his death, Gottlieb Daimler introduced the Daimler Phoenix to the market. Despite disputes regarding its performance, access to the passenger compartment, and body, this car started a new trend which is basically continued today. Wilhelm Maybach, the car's designer, resolved the cooling problem and designed a new four-cylinder engine mounted at the front. This 5 litre engine developed 17kW (23hp). Later on its power was increased to 25.7kW (35hp), and the car had a maximum speed of 75-80km/h (46-50mph). Among other innovations were a four-speed-and-reverse gearbox, honeycomb radiator, and pneumatic tyres. From that time cars were no longer fitted with solid tyres, but with pneumatic tyres of Dunlop, Michelin, or other continental make.

Gottlieb Daimler did not live to see the greatest success of his cars: he died in 1900.

MERCEDES SIMPLEX

1902

Manufactured by Daimler Motoren AG, Cannstatt, Germany

While the newly-established German motor companies such as Adler, Dixi or NAG made their debut with small models up to 7kW (10hp), the pioneer Daimler company continued production of powerful multi-cylinder vehicles.

Another example of the successful development of Daimler models was a new tourer, the Mercedes Simplex. Its designer, Wilhelm Maybach, incorporated many advanced features in it. The car was fitted with a 3050 cc front-mounted four-cylinder engine, with Bosch high-tension magneto system. The bore and stroke dimensions were 90×120mm. Its maximum power was 16.3kW (22hp) at 1200 rpm. Ballbearings were used instead of sliding bearings, and an accelerator pedal replaced a manual control. The model had also new engine lubrication and a four-speed-and-reverse gearbox. The drive was transmitted to the rear axle through chains, and the wheels were fitted with mechanical brakes. The elongated, low box-section chassis, short wheelbase, and a wider track gave a lower centre of gravity, resulting in better roadholding and comfort. The Mercedes Simplex weighed some 900kg (1980lb) and had a top speed of 80km/h (50mph).

Such a car was expected to have elegant, yet functional bodywork. The Simplex was manufactured in many styles, such as Tonneau, Doppel Tonneau, Phaeton, or Tourenwagen.

The sound and easy pronunciation of Mercedes gave this new name every chance to become famous internationally. Its reputation was increased by its participation in a number of international races in the early 1900s. W. K. Vanderbilt reached 111.106km/h (69mph) in his Mercedes Simplex in April 1902. This was a new world record for cars with petrol engines.

Mercedes Simplex was based on the modern concept of a car. Ever since, the box-section chassis and rigid bodywork, the engine and the radiator at the front, and seats at the rear, have been used in the majority of cars.

OLDSMOBILE CURVED DASH   1902

Manufactured by Olds Motor Works, Lansing, Michigan, USA

In 1900 the picture of America showed two worlds: that of the big towns and cities, linked by a rail network; and the smaller towns and villages ruled by the interests of the farmers. And it was actually the latter which influenced decisively the development of motoring, since farmers were more in need of cars than city-dwellers. Ransom Eli Olds realized this. It was he who provided the farmers with the first utility car.

After designing his first steam tricycle in 1893, Olds received financial support from a millionaire sawmill owner, and set up the Olds Motor Works in Detroit in 1897. After the failure of a gas-powered vehicle Olds signed a contract for a utility runabout, which had to be made in the shortest time possible. After production of the single-cylinder cars had begun the factory was destroyed by fire. Olds had to switch to an assembly-type production, using engines and chassis supplied by other companies. The cars were built at Lansing, Michigan.

In 1901 one of the most notable models of this trademark was designed, the Curved Dash two-seater with a short bogie-type chassis and a wheelbase of 1.676m (5ft 6in). The single-cylinder four-stroke engine developed 3.3kW (4.5hp). The vehicle weighed 320kg (700lb) and was fitted with a two-speed gearbox. This car was produced at the rate of 600 a year, and increased in 1904 to 5000. They were cheap but high-quality cars. But when Rey Chopin, the future director of the Hudson Motor Co. was driving an Oldsmobile to a New York show, the car almost fell apart. It took him 7½ days to reach New York. After he returned he tried to convince Olds that American roads needed bigger, heavier, and more expensive cars. Instead, Olds withdrew from the works, which became part of General Motors in 1908. He established his own REO company, the name being derived from the initial letters of Olds' name.

Oldsmobile featured several innovations. It was the first works to introduce mass production of cars, while the 1921 model 43 A was the first car fitted with forced cooling.

DE DION-BOUTON

Manufactured by de Dion-Bouton, Paris, France

Contemporaries of Count Albert de Dion, who was born in 1856, considered him an eccentric personality. His friends nicknamed him 'le Comte Sportif' since Albert de Dion was not only a skilful fencer but also one of the first motor drivers and founders of the French Motor Club.

Initially the de Dion-Bouton & Trépardoux company established in 1882, built steam-powered vehicles. As early as 1894 the Count had won the first Paris-Rouen car race with a steam tractor of his own design. After failing in the events that followed, he came to the conclusion that he petrol engine produced by Daimler of Stuttgart would do much better. His partner, Trépardoux thought this move would lead to bankruptcy, and cut himself adrift from the company. But even Daimler engines, with a 700-900 rpm range, could not satisfy de Dion, whose engines could run at 3000 rpm.

In 1895 de Dion-Bouton designed a small tricycle powered by a 0.55kW (¾hp) engine. Among its features were high-tension spark-plug ignition, a contact breaker, and an accumulator. Soon the vehicle became popular with the public, and over a hundred companies used this engine in their cars, including Renault, Delage, Phébus, Adler, and even Pierce Arrow in America.

At the 1899 Paris show the first 2.6kW (3.6hp) de Dion-Bouton Voiturette was exhibited.

The 1903 model shown here was fitted with a 942 cc single-cylinder engine developing 5.9kW (8hp). For several years it was the most popular French automobile. The two-speed gearbox was operated by a lever located beneath the steering wheel. The car weighed 310kg (683lb) and it could reach 45km/h (28mph). It was fitted with the unsprung de Dion rear axle, notable for its constant track and low weight. This axle was used mainly by the designers of racers and sports car, such as Alfa Romeo, Daimler-Benz, and Ferrari.

De Dion-Bouton, whose cars are exhibited in many European car museums, ceased to exist in 1933.

VAUXHALL   1905

Manufactured by Vauxhall Motors Ltd, Luton, Bedfordshire, England

The development of motoring in Britain gave rise to many clubs for motor drivers, designed to protect their interests.

The AA (Automobile Association) was established in 1903 for the protection of drivers against the police, who were very strict over infringements of the speed limit. By the Automobile Act of 1903 speed was limited to 36km/h (20mph). The AA organized patrols which warned drivers of police traps. Later the patrols were themselves equipped with cars and they acted as guides, rendered first aid in accidents and breakdowns, and provided other services. Organizing traffic, searching for stolen cars, and rendering first aid drew them closer to the police, leading to their co-operation.

The motoring craze which swept across the country in this way led the Vauxhall Iron Works to enlarge its production capacity and move to its present-day buildings at Luton in Bedfordshire. In 1905 the company was re-named Vauxhall Motors Ltd, and acquired an excellent designer, Laurence Pomeroy, who designed a car for the growing middle classes.

The car, shown opposite, was a smart two-seater, available at a reasonable price. The water-cooled engine had three cylinders, which was unusual, and developed 6.7kW (9hp). It was mounted beneath a hinged bonnet, typical of 1905 models. Other models that followed were fitted with the classical front radiator. The drive to the rear axle was transmitted from the front-mounted engine via a clutch and a three-speed gearbox. The 'classical' chassis with rigid axles had longitudinal leaf springs. This was also the first model in which Vauxhall used a steering wheel instead of a tiller. Emil Levassor, the French designer, driver, and motor company owner, invented the steering wheel as early as 1898.

Only 20 cars of this Vauxhall model were made and only one still exists. It is on show at Luton, together with other cars of the 1903-1930 period.

SPYKER   1906

Manufactured by Jacob and Hendrik Spijker, Trompenburg, Netherlands

From 1902 the brothers Jakobus and Hendrik Spijker ran the largest motor company in Holland. They employed a competent designer, Joseph Laviolette, who built the Spyker, a car that sold well, especially in England. In 1903-1905 Spyker's whole production was purchased by the Elsforth Automobile Company of Bradford. Spyker taxi cabs virtually flooded the streets of London.

The company did not neglect its advertising campaign. In 1907 Jakobus Spijker entered his car for the Peking-Paris race announced by *Le Matin*. Its driver was Charles Godard from Burgundy.

And so, on June 10, 1907, five vehicles, having been shipped to China, stood at the start in the old Imperial City. With difficulty the small convoy forced its way through the passes between Peking and Kalgan, squeezed through a 'hole' in the Great Wall of China, attacked the Gobi Desert and the Siberian tundra, and reached Paris after 61 days. The other cars were an Itala, two de Dions, and a Contal.

The Spyker in the race was a standard 15hp four-cylinder model. The cylinders were fitted in two blocks with a T-shaped head. With a bore and stroke of 90×100mm, the overall cylinder capacity was 2546 cc. The engine, with Spijker's patent pressure lubrication, developed 11-15kW (15-20hp) at 1000 rpm. The Longuemare carburettor was supplied with fuel from a tank beneath the front seat. The three-speed gearbox was fitted with roller bearings. Another useful innovation of Spijker's was a sprung steering wheel. The front band brake worked on the propeller shaft, the hand brake controlled the drum shoes of the rear wheels. The clutch was disengaged automatically when the brake was used. The frame was built from riveted steel sections. Godard used Michelin tyres for the trip. The car had a typical round radiator which was used on Spykers for the first time in 1905. After the race was over Spijker capitalized on the increased popularity he had gained by introducing a model with pneumatic transmission.

The company's last successful car was the 1921 model powered by a 5.7-litre six-cylinder Maybach engine developing 51.6kW (70hp). In 1927 the firm, which in the meantime had become involved in the aircraft industry, curtailed its production activity.

ITALA 35/45 HP

1907

Manufactured by Itala Fabbrica Automobili SA, Turin, Italy

In 1904 the Itala company was established in Turin. It was among the pioneers in car-design during the following decades, and its competitive successes made the newly established motor industry world famous.

The first Itala car was built by a talented designer, Matteo Ceirano. It was fitted with a 4502 cc four-cylinder engine developing 17.6kW (24hp). From the very beginning Ceirano strove to design a sports car. This became obvious at the Brescia Grand Prix, won by the 73.5kW (100hp) Itala 'Grand Prix'. This automobile was among the first in the world to use a propeller shaft for transmission instead of belts and chains.

Among the greatest victories which ensured Itala a place in the motoring history was the famous Peking-Paris race. Prince Scipione Borghese, his mechanic Ettore Guizzardi, and a journalist, Luigi Barzini, drove the 16,000 km (9942 mi) course in an Itala — and won. This strenuous and adventurous race lasted from June 10 to August 10, 1907.

The winning Itala, model 35/45 HP, was strictly a production car. It was fitted with an in-line four-cylinder engine with a bore and stroke of 130×140mm and a capacity of 7433 cc. The drive was transmitted to the rear axle via a bevel clutch and a four-speed gearbox. The front and rear axles were suspended on semi-elliptic leaf springs. The wooden-spoked wheels carried Pirelli pneumatic tyres. The coachwork was fitted with additional tanks and the mudguards were removed. Borghese carried a repair kit, a set of spare parts, and a dozen tyres and inner tubes.

This historic journey became the subject of several books. The original car is now exhibited at the Museo dell' Automobile Carlo Bisaretti di Ruffia in Turin.

In 1931 the company was re-named Itala SACA (Societa Anonyma Construzzioni Automobilistiche), but three years later the Itala disappeared owing to ever-increasing competition.

ROLLS-ROYCE SILVER GHOST   1907

Manufactured by Rolls-Royce Ltd, Manchester, England

The Rolls-Royce 'Silver Ghost', officially designated as Model 40/50 HP, owes this name to the journalists who watched the car's successful 24,140 km (15,000 mi) trial. The car, which was fitted with a silver-painted body and adorned with a mahogany dashboard, was tested by members of the RAC (Royal Automobile Club). Its exceptionally quiet engine and a maximum speed of 120km/h (75mph), foreshadowed the fame of this British firm.

The trial, on rough country roads between Glasgow and London, lasted for 48 days. After the tests were over, the technical committee of the RAC dismantled the car for examination, and then a certificate was issued which in 1906 was of a greater significance than any advertisement whatsoever. Good evidence of this is the total number of 6,173 cars manufactured between 1907 and 1925. This car was also built under licence by Rolls-Royce of America, Inc, in Springfield, Massachusetts.

The Rolls-Royce Silver Ghost shown here had a 7036 cc six-cylinder in-line engine with two cylinder blocks. The compression ratio was 3.2, with identical bore and stroke of 114mm. The side-valve engine, with an L-shaped cylinder head, had a crankshaft carried in seven bearings, and it had double ignition with two independent circuits and two sparking plugs per cylinder. This engine, with a duplex carburettor of Royce's own design, could develop 35.3kW (48hp) at 1200 rpm. The car was fitted with a four-speed gate-type gearbox.

The classical chassis with reinforced oblong frame carried the rigid axles on semi-elliptic leaf springs, with friction shock-absorbers. Mechanical brakes operated on the rear wheels only. The chassis alone weighed 1200kg (2646lb). It was supplied either in long or short versions, with three wheelbase dimensions. Various bodies were mounted on the chassis, styled by famous contemporary bodymakers such as Mulliner, Barker, or the American Brewster. The Montagu Motor Museum at Beaulieu, Hampshire, boasts one of the largest Rolls-Royce collections.

THOMAS FLYER 6-70   1907

Manufactured by E.R. Thomas Motor Co, Buffalo, New York, USA

On February 12, 1908, the anniversary of President Abraham Lincoln's birthday, some 50,000 people gathered in New York City. They were there not to celebrate Lincoln's birthday, but the start of the New York-Paris run covering 2092 km (13,000 mi) across three continents.

Six automobiles started in the race: the American Thomas, the German Protos, the Italian Zust, and three French entrants — de Dion, Motobloc, and Sizaire Naudin. The winner of this venturesome marathon, which included a run across Siberia, was George Schuster in his Thomas Flyer 6-70. He covered the distance in 168 days.

The victorious car was built by Erwin Ross Thomas. In 1900-1902, having previously made engines and motorcycles, the company embarked on car production. From 1902, when the first twin-cylinder was produced, the company gradually went from three- and four- up to six-cylinder engines. From 1905 the cars were sold under the name Thomas Flyer.

The 6-70 Thomas model pictured was fitted with a six-cylinder square engine with bore and stroke dimensions of 140×140mm. The engine had a capacity of 12,936 cc. The engine power of 52.9kW (72hp) was transmitted through a four-speed gearbox to the rear axle via a propeller shaft. The less powerful Thomas Touring model used chains for the rear wheel drive.

From 1909 Thomas ran our of luck, and Eugen Meyer became interested in the company. But even he could not save this manufacturer of quality cars from deterioration. In 1919 the Thomas cars came to an end.

FORD MODEL T   1908

Manufactured by Ford Motor Co, Detroit, Michigan, USA

The company established by Henry Ford in 1903 as the Ford Motor Co. made a wide range of models: A, B, C, F, K, N, and R, fitted with twin-, four-, and even six-cylinder engines. Ford steadily improved materials and designs in order to achieve the best possible strength and the lowest weights, and finally he developed the famous Model T. In 1908 the car was designed by Ford's engineer, Harold C. Wills. He fitted it with an in-line water-cooled engine, with a capacity of 2898 cc developing 17.6kW (24hp) at 1800 rpm. It had side valves. The John Heinz magneto flywheel generated power even at very low revolutions. When starting, the ignition coil was connected to a dry battery. Another novelty was the two-speed epicyclic gearbox fitted to a flywheel and operated by a pedal, and hand brakes. The 'Tin Lizzie', as the car was called by customers, was all steel. The mechanisms were waterproof. It was roomy and wide, with good roadholding. Its overhead clearance and low weight made it suitable for any terrain. When testing the car in 1910 technicians of the British RAC observed that its 6583kg (14,513lb) weight was equally distributed on both axles. The car could drive in one gear from as low as 10.8km/h (6mph) to a maximum speed of 63km/h (39mph).

In 1909 Henry Ford decided to produce one, and only one, car, and that was Model T. He eliminated manual work in car production, and stated that the chassis in all cars would be identical.

In the season of 1909-1910 some 18,664 cars were sold for $950 each. A year later the figure increased to 34,528 cars costing $780 each. As production rose the price fell. In 1913 Ford introduced assembly-line production. In 1916-1917 as many as 785,432 of these cars were sold at $360 each. The Model T had virtually flooded America. In 1923 the daily output reached 10,000, and in 1927, when the production of this, Ford's most popular model came to an end, the overall number of cars produced had reached 15,007,033.

The reliability of the engine and the gearbox, the excellent resistance to bad driving and rough terrain, made the 'Tin Lizzie' popular the world over.

RENAULT AX 1909

Manufactured by Société Renault Fréres, Billancourt, France

In 1906 Renault won the ACF Grand Prix, organized by the Automobile Club de France — (ACF). This event was the first Grand Prix in the world. The winning car, driven by Franz Szisz, was fitted with a 12.8-litre four-cylinder engine developing 77.7kW (105hp). Its maximum speed was 148.5km/h (92mph). This victory was the firm's best advertisement, and in 1906 Renault's production exceeded 2000 cars for the first time. The Renault trademark soon became popular beyond the French border. The twin-cylinder version was exported to Britain.

The Renault AX was powered by an in-line twin-cylinder engine with a bore and stroke of 100×120mm and a capacity of 1885 cc. This SV engine developed 10.3kW (14hp) at 1600 rpm. Ignition was provided by a high-tension magneto system. The engine was water-cooled, with the radiator mounted traditionally behind the engine and the fan in the flywheel. The three-speed gearbox transmitted the drive to the rigid rear axle via a bevel clutch. The bodywork was attached to a longitudinal frame, and it was carried on semi-elliptic leaf springs. The hand brake operated on the rear wheels. This 860kg (1895lb) car had a top speed of 65km/h (40mph).

The modified AG model with the driver outside, passengers within, became a popular taxicab in Paris. These vehicles played a leading role on the outbreak of the First World War in 1914. By late August German troops had crossed the Marne. The French military headquarters feared they could not defend Paris against the invasion. Suddenly an idea struck the military governor of Paris, General Joseph Galliéni — to mobilize all usable Paris taxis to speed reinforcements to the 6th Army under General Michel Maunory, which was in a position to make a flanking counter-attack. So on the morning of September 2, 700 taxi cabs of the G7 model (red) and G3 (green) transported 3000 men to the 6th Army. Each vehicle accommodated four soldiers and a driver. Thus reinforced, Maunory's counterattack saved Paris from capitulation. Afterwards the AG model was nicknamed 'the Marne Taxi'. Several of these vehicles are exhibited at the Hôtel des Invalides in Paris.

LE ZÉBRE, MODEL 'A'   1909

Manufactured by SA Le Zèbre, Suresnes, Puteaux, Seine, France

As a result of a meeting of two talented designers, Jules Salomon and Lamy, a new French trademark, Le Zèbre, was announced. The company began production in 1909 with a trial series of lightweight vehicles, the forerunners of the later legendary Citröen 5 CV Trèfle.

The car was powered by a 616 cc side-valve engine. It was a single-cylinder water-cooled engine with bore and stroke dimensions of 85×106mm, developing 4.4kW (6hp). Ignition was provided by a high-tension magneto system. Power to the rear wheels was transmitted via a propeller shaft through a multiple disc clutch and a two-speed gearbox. The rigid axles were mounted on semi-elliptic springs. The brakes controlled the rear wheels only. The A model, with its light two-seater body, weighed 350kg (770lb) and achieved a maximum speed of 45km/h (28mph).

The following year the improved B model was announced, fitted with a four-speed gearbox and a four-seater body.

The C series, produced from 1911 to 1914 with a 'teardrop' body, was fitted with a 785 cc four-cylinder engine. The vehicle developed 4.4kW (6hp), and was the smallest production four-cylinder.

Salomon designed his last Zèbre in 1919, and joined Citröen, for whom he had worked before. In the meantime Lamy established his own Amilcar Co.

In the early 1920s Le Zèbre Co. realized that the market was interested in large cars, and so abandoned production of the little Zebras. Its new models had 2000 cc four-cylinder engines. Among the best known was the Z model. However, the company never achieved the success it expected owing to financial constraints, and stopped production in 1930.

ARGYLL 12 HP   1910

Manufactured by Argyll Motor Ltd, Alexandria, Strathclyde, Scotland

The Scottish motor company established in Glasgow by Alex Govan produced cars from 1899. Initially the firm was called Hozier's Engineering Co, and applied Renault engineering practice. Its first Voiturette was fitted with a 318 cc engine, a propeller shaft, and a tubular frame. The engine developed 2kW (2.7hp). A more powerful model fitted with an 864 cc engine was also made. A few years later a four-speed gearbox model was on the market.

Beside the main factory in Glasgow a new works was built in the nearby town of Alexandria in 1905. The company name was changed to Argyll Motor Ltd.

The advancement of the new Scottish trademark was epitomized in the 1910 12hp model, using front-wheel braking for the first time. The expander cam was fitted on top, according to the design of the French engineer Henri Perrot.

Even though front brakes cut the braking distance almost by 60 per cent, this novelty had been eyed suspiciously by its opponents for a long time. The public was still influenced by unfortunate experiences with the bicycle, and thought front-wheel braking might make the car turn over. Experts published warning articles in motoring papers. Designers were concerned rather with the negative effect of heavy front brakes on steering, and so many motor companies waited until 1925 when Rolls-Royce decided to fit front wheel brakes. The next Argyll 15/30 HP and 25/50 HP models were fitted with brakes on all wheels.

At that time Argyll offered ten different models fitted with sleeve-valve engines. These engines differed from Knight's engine in that they were fitted with a steel Burt-McCollum sleeve-valve which turned and slid simultaneously, thus opening and closing the inlet and exhaust pipes. After a dispute over the patent of the sleeve-valve engine, Govan got into financial difficulties, which he overcame thanks to the racing success of his 15/30 HP model. For 14 hours a Argyll 15/30 HP lapped the Brooklands circuit at an average speed of 128km/h (80mph), thus setting a record for the track.

Although the company carried on production until 1932, its postwar models were less popular.

BUICK 24/30 HP   1911

Manufactured by Buick Motor Co, Flint, MIchigan, USA

David Dunbar Buick was born at Arbroath in Scotland. At the age of two he moved with his parents to Detroit. At 16 he became a plumber, and later on he and some friends set up the Buick and Sherwood Manufacturing Company, producing water closets. However, Buick was keen to build motor-cars, so in 1902 he sold his share in the plumbing venture and joined James H. Whitting, who owned a carriage factory in Flint, not far from Detroit, and who also planned to make cars. The new company was named the Buick Motor Company, although most of the shares belonged to Whitting.

In July 1904 the first Buick was produced, and was designated as the B model. It was fitted with a 2.6 litre horizontally-opposed twin-cylinder engine. At its maximum of 1200 rpm it developed a respectable 16.2kW (22hp). This model, an open four-seater without a windscreen, had a top speed of 56km/h (35mph). The B model's price included the horn, acetylene lamps, a repair kit, and a blanket for working under the car.

Although the B model sold well, production problems put the company into such financial difficulties that additional capital was needed to keep the firm running. The necessary $300,000 were contributed by William Crapo Durant, who had bought up other car companies, such as Olds Motor Works, Oakland, and Cadillac. Thus in 1908 a new firm was started, the General Motors Company..

Buick became an independent trademark within the GMC. In 1911 it announced its new 24/30 HP model, a five-seater. The vehicle was fitted with a 4337 cc in-line four-cylinder engine. Power was transmitted to the rigid rear axle via a multiple disc clutch and a two-speed gearbox. The engine was water-cooled. The chassis, with an extremely rigid frame, was carried on semi-elliptic springs at the front and elliptic springs at the rear.

ALFA 12 HP 1911

Manufactured by Anonima Lombarda Fabbrica Automobili, Milan, Italy

In Italian, Alfa is not only the first letter of the Greek alphabet (alpha) but also an abbreviation of Anonima Lombarda Fabbrica Automobili, which was established in 1909 by the purchase of Darracq's Societa Italiana Automobili Darracq in Portello, in the Milanese suburbs. In 1915 the factory was bought by industrialist Nicola Romeo and after the First World War the company's name was changed to Alfa Romeo.

In the 1911-1912 period the first Alfa racers were entered for the famous Targa Florio circuit. Targa Florio bears the name of the founder of this race, Vincenzo Florio — a member of an influential Sicilian family — who had donated a massive gold shield trophy, the Targa. In 1906 the first race was held on a twisty track 146 km (90 ml) long, with a 1210m (4000ft) altitude difference and 1006 bends. It was a race for standard sports cars. It was won by Alessandro Cagno in an Itala at an average speed of 46.8km/h (29mph). The driver and his mechanic did all the work — changed the tyres, filled up with oil, petrol, and water, replaced the plugs, and the like. The race covered some nine hours of driving. Alfa Romeo held a unique record in this event by six consecutive victories from 1930 to 1935.

The first ALFA was a 24hp model fitted with a 4084 cc engine, a gearbox, and a propeller shaft, and built in 1910.

The 1911 12 hp model shown here was inspired by the 24 hp model. The 2414 cc engine had bore and stroke of 80×120mm. With its three-speed gearbox it developed 8.8kW (12hp). It was made in three versions fitted with 22 CV, 25 CV, and 28 CV engines. The car's maximum speed was 90-100km/h (56-62mph). It was produced either in a limousine version or with 'teardrop' coachwork weighing 920kg (2030lb). The sports derivative of the 12 hp took part in the Primo Concorso di Regolarita di Modena event, which was split into five sections with an overall distance of 1500 km (932 mi).

The total number of these cars built between 1910 and 1915 was 330.

SCANIA-VABIS 18/20 HP   1911

Manufactured by AS Scania-Vabis, Sodertälje, Sweden

When it started the Malmö Maskinfabriks AB Scania company made
Humber bicycles under licence, but in 1902 it embarked on the
production of light cars. Its first vehicle, fitted with a tonneau body,
was powered by a twin-cylinder engine supplied by Heinrich Kämper, a
Berlin manufacturer. The gearbox was connected to the engine by a
chain drive. This model was used by Sweden's Crown Prince Gustav
(later King Gustavus V) for several years.

The AB Vabis company, established in Sodertälje in 1891,
specialized in building railway carriages, but its engineer, Gustav
Erikson, designed his first Vabis automobile as early as 1897. The
vehicle was fitted with a two-stroke twin-cylinder engine with hot-
tube ignition. Meanwhile, the company was making its money with
commercial vehicles. AB Vabis and AB Scania merged in 1911.

The newly-established company began production with the Scania-
Vabis 18/20 HP. The car was powered by a four-cylinder in-line
2270 cc engine with bore and stroke of 85×100mm. The power was
transmitted through a four-speed gearbox to the rear axle. Both rigid
axles were carried on semi-elliptic leaf springs. It was in production for
just one year.

After the First World War, Scania-Vabis extended its production of
trucks and commercial vehicles. The company manufactured trucks,
fire-engines, mail vans, and other vehicles with special bodies.

Because of a drop in the demand for vehicles in the late 1920s the
last passenger car left the factory in 1929, and Scania and Vabis went
back to their original production programmes. Scania continued
producing bicycles within the Saab company, and Vabis carried on
making railway carriages.

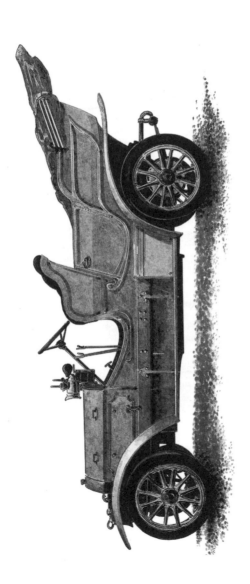

FIAT ZERO   1912

Manufactured by Fiat SA, Turin, Italy

Before the outbreak of the First World War European car
manufacturers began mass-production, following the example of
Henry Ford in Detroit. The Fiat company was not among the passive
onlookers. As early as 1910 the prototypes of the future Fiat Zero had
been seen in the streets of Turin. They were first introduced on the
market as late as 1912, when the assembly lines and modified
conditions of volume production had been well run in.

Although the Fiat Zero followed the '1' model, it was shorter than its
predecessor — hence the name Zero. This car, thanks to its
performance, realiabiity, longevity, and low price, was highly favoured
by the public. The Zero was fitted with a 15hp four-cylinder in-line
1846 cc engine, with bore and stroke of 70×120mm. The drive to the
rear axle was transmitted via a four-speed gearbox and a propeller
shaft. The chassis was supported on longitudinal semi-elliptic springs
at the front and quarter-elliptic springs at the rear.

The first models were sold in the 'teardrop' version. By 1915 2041
had been built.

One necessity for mass-production was strict standardization of all
materials and prefabricated sections. Thanks to the standardization
introduced in the production of this model, the use of different kinds of
steel was cut down to one third, out of a thousand steel tubes only 36
were used, and 52 bearings instead of several hundred. This simplified
supply, storage, and assembly procedures.

In 1915 an improved version of the Zero model was announced,
fitted with a more powerful engine developing 14kW (19hp) at
2000 rpm. This car had electric lighting. It weighed 900kg (1980lb)
and had a top speed of 62km/h (39mph). The company provided a
chassis fitted with either Spider or Laudaulet coachwork. A
windscreen was among the novelties introduced in this model. Until
then drivers had regarded this as unnecessary, since it obstructed the
view on a nice day and was a nuisance when it rained.

HISPANO-SUIZA ALFONSO   1912

Manufactured by Hispano-Suiza SA, Barcelona, Spain

The first Hispano-Suiza Alfonso models — not then known by that name — were built as early as 1910 by the founder of the company, the young Swiss engineer Marc Birkigt. He capitalized on design ideas which only later became generally accepted in motoring industry, such as a T-shaped cylinder head and aluminium engine block with inserted cylinders.

The 1912 Alfonso model was powered by an in-line, four-cylinder water-cooled 3622 cc engine, which owed its unusual flexibility to an incredibly long stroke — 200mm — compared with the 75mm bore. It developed 47kW (65hp) at 2300 rpm, and this power was transmitted through a three-speed Hotchkiss gearbox via a propeller shaft to the rear rigid axle. The oblong frame was supported on semi-elliptic longitudinal leaf springs in the front and three-quarter elliptics at the rear. The mechanical brakes operated on the rear wheels only. The Rudge-and-Whitworth spoked wheels were fixed to finely grooved central hubs. The car had a top speed of 120km/h (75mph) which was remarkable in those days.

Hispano-Suiza was very enthusiastic about entering for races. The Spanish king, Alfonso XIII, was an ardent promotor of motoring and an excellent racing driver. At the steering wheel of this model he entered the 1912 San Sebastian-Madrid race and set a new record on the course. After that the car was named after him and it became the most famous Hispano-Suiza sports car.

At the outbreak of the First World War Hispano-Suiza started production as a factory at Bois-Colombes, near Paris. The works was already known for its excellent V8 aero-engines, used in American, British, and French fighters. The slightly modified Alfonso model produced by Hispano-Suiza was slotted into the production programme of the French car manufacturer.

Production also continued at the Spanish plant in Barcelona, which made this luxurious sports car as late as 1920.

MORRIS OXFORD   1912

Manufactured by Morris Motors Ltd, Oxford, England

For some years William Morris sold and repaired cars from his garage in Longwall, Oxford, and this gave him a good idea of the designs of different makes, among them Arrol-Johnson, Belsize, Enfield, Humber, Hupmobil, Singer, Standard, and Wolseley. He compared their production technology, and in 1910 he embarked on producing his own vehicle, which he then called Morris Oxford. What Morris had in mind was an economy vehicle with low running and maintenance costs, using a great number of parts obtained from outside suppliers.

The prototype Morris Oxford, without an engine, was built at Morris's garage in Oxford in 1912. Later the cars were assembled at a former military training college at Cowley, which Morris bought cheaply. This first car incorporated a 1080 cc four-cylinder White & Poppe engine, with bore and stroke of 60×90mm; a three-speed gearbox, also produced by White & Poppe; Sankey wheels; Dunlop tyres; and Powell & Hammer headlights. It was claimed that 'Morris' is the only light car which embodies the joint production of the greatest British experts.' Despite some setbacks in the engine cooling system and steering, with rather poor roadholding, the Morris Oxford managed to establish its position in the market. This was achieved by its fairly good performance, reliability, and low running costs. From 1913 to 1917 Morris built 1475 of these cars.

However, the Morris Oxford could not win a larger market since a two-seater body was as much as the engine output could handle. The car could not compete with four-seater family cars. In order to satisfy this demand Morris developed a new larger version, the Cowley model, also called the Bullnose Morris because of the shape of its radiator.

STUTZ BEARCAT   1912

Manufactured by Ideal Motor Car, Indianapolis, Indiana, USA

The name of this American firm is linked with successes on the Indianapolis track. The company was established in 1911 under the name of Ideal Motor Car. It was founded by Harry D. Stutz, who came to fame in the first Indianapolis 500, in which he drove a sports car fitted with a 5000 cc four-cylinder Wisconsin engine.

In 1912, after the company had been renamed Stutz, it announced its new Bearcat model, which was soon among the most popular American sports cars of the period. The Bearcat was fitted with a 6396 cc four-cylinder water-cooled engine developing 44.1kW (60hp) at 1500 rpm. It was a typical racer, without bodywork in the true sense of the word, fitted with a long bonnet, two anatomic seats, and a 'Monocle Windshield' for the driver only. The car's rear consisted of a giant fuel tank and two spare tyres. Among the design novelties was the connection of a three-speed gearbox to a differential on the rear axle. This is known as the transaxle arrangement, and has been revived in recent years.

In 1926 Stutz introduced his sensational 'safety Stutz', fitted with hydraulic brakes on all four wheels. The in-line eight-cylinder engine, with camshaft in the cylinder head, developed 67.7mW (92hp) at 3200 rpm. Among other features were the centrally lubricated chassis and a windshield. With every purchase the company also arranged for free insurance of the crew for one year.

In the early 1930s Stutz tried to make his mark in the range of luxury cars. He developed the DV model, which stood for Dual Valves. It was an eight-cylinder with four valves per cylinder and a top speed of 160km/h (100mph). But the commercial failure of this car spelled the end for Stutz.

DARRACQ 13 1913

Manufactured by Société A. Darracq, Suresnes, France

In the late 1800s a large number of car companies were established in France, among them Berliet, Darracq, Décauville, de Dietrich, and Mors.

In 1897 Alexander Darracq established the Sociéte A. Darracq. His cars, produced at Suresnes, played an important rôle in helping other car companies to get launched. Darracq had agencies in Britain, Italy, and Germany. The Opel brothers were the first German car entrepreneurs producing the Opel-Darracq vehicle under French licence. In 1909 the Italian Darracq agency became a new company, Anonima Lombarda Fabbrica Automobili, manufacturing a wide range of models under the ALFA trademark. After the First World War it was known as Alfa Romeo.

Darracq was the first company to design a car with an eight-cylinder engine. This was the Grande Voiture Darracq, built in 1905, which was destined to break speed records. The car had a 22.5 litre V8-engine with bore and stroke of 160×140mm, developing 137kW (200hp) at 1200 rpm.

The 1904 Darracq was the heroine of the movie *Généviève*. This film, made in 1952, was based on the annual 'oldtimer' London-Brighton run. The central 'character' of the film was a Darracq automobile, a two-seater fitted with a twin-cylinder engine developing 8.8kW (12hp). It was lent by Norman Reeves, a car businessman, afterwards nicknamed 'Mr. Généviève'.

In 1913 the company produced the Darracq 13, having a 1.4 litre four-cylinder in-line engine. The car developed 9.6kW (13hp) and had a top speed of 70km/h (43mph). The chassis, with rigid axles was suspended on semi-elliptic springs.

The last Darracq was sold in 1928. Then the firm merged with the French Talbot and British Sunbeam, and the STD motor company was established.

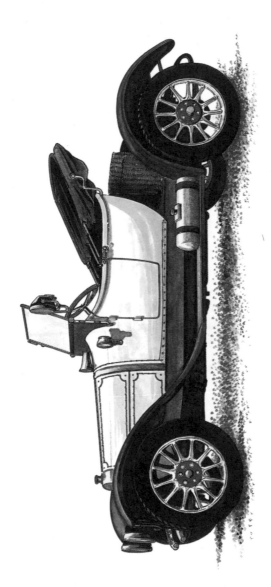

Manufactured by Gräf & Stift, Automobilfabrik AG, Vienna, Austria

The Gräf brothers, Carl, Franz and Heinrich, owned a bicycle repair shop in Vienna, and as early as 1895 they built a car which was one of the first with front-wheel drive. The Gräf Voiturette was fitted with a single-cylinder de Dion-Bouton 402 cc engine developing 2.6kW (3.5hp). It had a two-speed gearbox. The power was transmitted to the front axle shaft by a propellor shaft via a differential.

On November 1, 1901 the Gräf brothers joined with the former textile entrepreneur Wilhelm Stift and started making automobiles, which were sold under the Spitz trademark until 1907. Arnold Spitz was a Viennese businessman dealing in cars, and also the most important partner in the firm. The company concentrated on the production of big, reliable, and luxurious cars, often referred to as the Austrian Rolls-Royces.

In 1913 Gräf und Stift designed a model with a 5.8 litre four-cylinder engine developing 23.5kW (32hp). It was in one of these cars that, on June 28, 1914, the successor to the Austrian throne, Archduke Franz Ferdinand, was assassinated in Sarajevo. This vehicle remained the property of Emperor Franz Joseph until 1916. Sixty years later it was bought back by Gräf und Stift.

After the First World War Gräf und Stift introduced what was in its time among the biggest automobiles. Its 7.8 litre, six-cylinder ohv engine developed 80.9kW (110hp) at 2400 rpm. It had twin Zenith carburettors. This giant, with wood-spoked wheels, weighed 2000kg (4400lb). Even bigger was the SP 8 model of the early 1930s. This vehicle, with the lion emblem of Gräf und Stift on the radiator grille, had an eight-cylinder engine developing 92.4kW (125hp). This limousine weighed 2500kg (5500lb).

Gräf und Stift stopped making cars in 1938, and limited its production to trucks.

PEUGEOT BÉBÉ

Manufactured by SA des Automobiles Peugeot, Sochaux, France

Peugeot capitalized on the new wave of fashionable small, lightweight vehicles by designing its Peugeot 6 PS Bébé, announced in 1901. This 270kg (595lb) cyclecar was not even fitted with reverse. Its name, Bébé, was also used for later Peugeot cars.

The 1905 6 PS Bébé was the first car to use shock-absorbers. They were invented by Armand Peugeot. It had a 695 cc single-cylinder water-cooled four-stroke engine, developing 4.4kW (6hp) at 1000 rpm. The drive was transmitted to the rigid rear axle by means of a leather-lined cone clutch, a gearbox, and a propeller shaft. The wooden body was fitted to a tubular steel chassis frame. The whole vehicle weighed 550kg (1200lb).

In 1912 a new series of Bébés was introduced, designed by the then unknown Ettore Bugatti. The in-line four-cylinder 856 cc engine had bore and stroke of 55×90mm, and an output sufficient for the car's weight of 330kg (730lb). The drive was transmitted via a two-speed gearbox. Reverse was engaged by a separate lever. The car had a top speed of 60km/h (37mph). The front rigid axle was supported on transverse semi-elliptic springs. The biggest problem was the tyres, which wore away fast and needed to be replaced every 10,000km (6200 mi). Another drawback was the imprecise steering. Despite these imperfections the Bébé was produced until 1916, and a total of 3095 cars were built. Later, the Bébé was replaced by the Quadrilette, the design of which showed its descent from the Bébé. Its commercial success is evident because more than 100,000 were produced.

RUSSO-BALT K 1913

Manufactured by Russko-Baltskij vagonnyj zavod, Riga, Russia

Russian cars appeared almost at the same time as Italian, English and American. The first was exhibited at the All-Russian Arts and Crafts Exhibition in Nizhny Novgorod (now Gorky) in May 1896. It was a two-seater 'horseless carriage' with a single-cylinder engine developing 1.1kW (1.5hp). The vehicle weighed 300kg (660lb) and it had a maximum speed of 20km/h (12mph). It was manufactured by two companies: the P. Freze carriage-manufacturing workshop and the E. Yakovlev engine factory. At that time foreign cars were being imported into Russia, among them Benz, Adler, and Panhard-Levassor, or were manufactured under licence, such as de Dion-Bouton, Daimler Cannstatt, and La Buire, and therefore nobody was much interested in a Russian-made car.

In 1908, however, car production began at the Russian-Baltic plant in Riga. The factory's production capacity was between 100 and 140 vehicles a year. There were four pasenger models: model K with a 17.6kW (24hp) engine, model E with 25.7kW (35hp), model S with 29.4kW (40hp) and a 44.1kW (60hp) model. The firm also made three truck models, and special versions, such as the 1915 half-track Russo-Balt, specially designed for military purposes.

André Nagel, editor of the *Automobil*, entered for the 1912 Monte Carlo Rally at the wheel of a Russo-Balt K. The 3257 km (2024 mi) race started in St. Petersburg (now Leningrad). After it was over Nagel reported that the car had slipped off the road about 40 times owing to thick snow and he had had to use the so-called *anti-dérapant* (anti-skid). This was a leather belt studded with nails which fitted over a tyre. Nagel, who had to drive his car for 3000 km (1860 mi) from Paris to St. Petersburg before the race, came ninth, but the magazine acknowledged him as the real winner.

In 1922 Russo-Balt production was moved to Moscow.

VAUXHALL PRINCE HENRY   **1914**

Manufactured by Vauxhall Motors Ltd, Luton, Bedfordshire, England

The Vauxhall Iron Works was established by a young Scottish mechanic, Alexander Wilson, at Vauxhall in South London in 1857. The first car was made there in 1903. Two years later the factory was moved to Luton in Bedfordshire, where Vauxhall Motors Ltd was established, and car production began under the watchful eye of designer Laurence Pomeroy.

The firm's first success came in 1908 when a Vauxhall sports car won a 320 km (200 mi) race. A Vauxhall was also the first car to exceed 160km/h (100mph) at Brooklands.

In 1911 Pomeroy designed the Prince Henry, named after the Prince Henry events in Germany. This car had a 3969 cc in-line four-cylinder engine with side valve arrangement and a four-speed gearbox. It developed 55.2kW (75hp) at 2500 rpm. It was fitted with semi-elliptic leaf springs and cantilever suspension at the rear. It could reach 120km/h (75mph). A sports version took part in the 1913 Shelsley Walsh, Worcestershire, hill climb. The car broke all records, and the perfected 30/98 Vauxhall model entered motoring history. It was in production until 1927.

In 1926 Vauxhall merged with General Motors. During the First World War the factory manufactured trucks and tanks. After the war the firm entered a period of boom, with more factories established at Luton, Ellesmere Port, and Dunstable. The company installed a trial track at Luton to simulate all driving conditions.

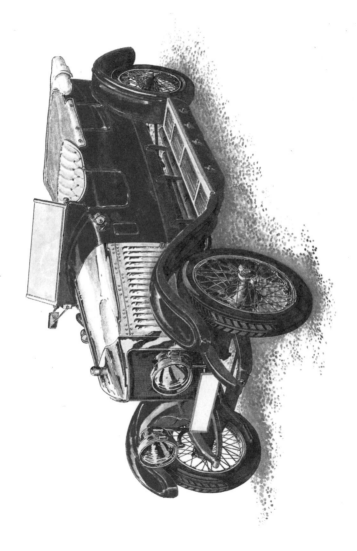

PIERCE-ARROW

Manufactured by Pierce-Arrow Motor Co, Buffalo, New York, USA

Pierce-Arrow cars were made by one of the most advanced American motor companies. The works was established in 1901 by George N. Pierce at Buffalo, NY, where he owned a bicycle factory which also produced household utensils. There he made his first Pierce-Motorette. The vehicle was fitted with a single-cylinder water-cooled engine, produced under licence from de Dion. But Pierce did not make small vehicles for long. His aim was to build bigger and more expensive cars, following the example of other American firms. In 1904 he announced the Great Arrow 24/48. This car had a 4400 cc four-cylinder engine, which was a sensation.

In 1909 Pierce enhanced the sports character of his cars by including the Arrow sign in the company's emblem. From then on the company was known as the Pierce-Arrow Motor Car Co.

In 1913 Pierce-Arrow introduced a novelty, headlights sunk into the mudguards. In those days, however, this was not for streamlining, just a quest for a unique shape. If customers preferred, the company also supplied cars with 'classical' headlights.

The 1919 Pierce-Arrow is a typical representative of the luxury range in which the company had firmly established its position. It had an in-line, six-cylinder, 8577 cc water-cooled engine, with bore and stroke of 114.3×139.7mm. It developed 55.2kW (75hp) at 2500 rpm. The cylinders were fitted in three blocks of two with a side-valve arrangement. Ignition was doubled: each cylinder had two plugs. The drive was transmitted to the rear wheels through a four-speed gearbox. The chassis, with two rigid axles, was suspended on semi-elliptic springs at the front and three quarter-elliptic springs at the rear.

The Pierce-Arrow cars stayed popular until 1922 when the company faced financial difficulties because of falling car prices. In 1928 the company merged tentatively with Studebaker.

CITRÖEN B2

1921

Manufactured by SA André Citröen, Paris, France

In 1900 André Citröen established a factory producing special gear wheels. Later on the company's emblem was two meshed gear wheels. After the First World War the firm began building cars.

The A model was the company's first car. Its design was in many respects based on Citröen's experience with American technology. The majority of machines used in the production lines had been shipped over from America. In July 1919 the 'teardrop' four-seater with three doors had its première. It was powered by a 1327 cc in-line four-cylinder engine with bore and stroke of 65×100mm. It developed 13.2kW (18hp) at 2100 rpm and had a top speed of 65km/h (42mph). Comfort was ensured by its long wheelbase. Novel features included an electric starter — highly appreciated by the ladies — electric lighting, and a complete spare wheel, which saved work in fitting and pumping up a new tyre.

The B model was announced in April 1921. It had a more powerful engine.. The bore was enlarged to 68mm, the capacity was raised to 1452 cc, and the power went up to 14.7kW (20hp) at 2100 rpm. The drive was transmitted to the rear rigid axle through a three-speed gearbox. With a weight of 850kg (1870lb) the car could reach 70km/h (44mph). The Citröen B2 was made in many versions until 1926, and altogether some 90,000 were built.

In 1921 André Citröen introduced the most successful of his small cars, the C3, also called Tréfle (Trefoil) because of its seating arrangement. The Tréfle was powered by a relatively small 855 cc engine. Soon it became the most popular model of its time and, considering driving conditions then, it had a relatively good performance with a maximum speed of 60km/h (37mph). The drive was transmitted from the four-cylinder engine to the rear axle via a three-speed gearbox. The engine developed 8.1kW (11hp). By 1926 over 80,000 C3s had been sold.

ALFA ROMEO RL SPORT   1922

Manufactured by SA Alfa Romeo, Milan, Italy

Shortly after the First World War Alfa Romeo embarked on a racing programme as its best advertising campaign. Thanks to the excellent designs of Giuseppe Merosi and Vittorio Jaňo, and first-class drivers such as Alberto Ascari, Giuseppe Campari, Tazio Nuvolari, Louis Chiron, and Achille Varzi, Alfa Romeos scored many successes.

Among the earliest racers was the Alfa Romeo RL. The 2994 cc in-line six-cylinder engine developed a power of 61kW (84hp). It was the brainchild of a surveyor, Giuseppe Merosi. This was an outstanding example of a car which was not the work of a professional designer. The RL was made both in touring and sports versions. Cars of the first and second series had brakes fitted to the rear wheels only. The third series, announced in 1923, had brakes on all four wheels. The touring version had a top speed of 115km/h (70mph), the sports model as much as 150km/h (93mph). Between 1923 and 1927 this model won 90 victories in the GT category. In 1929 came the sixth series, the RL Super Sport. By 1934 some 2579 had been built. The RL Sport shown here was styled by the Castagna bodymaking firm.

From 1924 the factory used supercharged engines in its racers. The experience gained in this way led the firm to fit superchargers to its six-cylinder production cars. The beautiful 1750 model and the successful 8C 2300 foreshadowed the early 1930s when Alfa Romeo became the No. 1 name on the race track.

In 1933, owing to financial constraints, the company withdrew from racing. The newly-developed cars were given to the company's former driver, Enzo Ferrari, who later set up Scuderio Ferrari in Modena.

RENAULT 9 L   1922

Manufactured by SA des Usines Renault, Billancourt, France

The Monte Carlo Rally is one of the most important international contests. Since the first one in 1911 the rules have changed several times. In that first rally points could be awarded for the following:

The greatest distance from a standing start from 12 specified points;

Average speed, the minimum being 10km/h /6mph) — this included a stop-over for the night and border crossings;

Number of passengers;

Comfort. The jury awarded points according to their own discretion. even windows were awarded points — the more windows the better score;

Technical condition: at the starting point the coachwork, engine and chassis were sealed.

In 1925 the winner was a Renault driven by François Repousseau. It was powered by a 9121 cc six-cylinder engine. This six-metre (20ft) long Renault was among the most luxurious sports cars of the 1920s. Politicians, industrialists, and film stars favoured it. With a power of 104kW (140hp) it achieved a then almost unbelievable maximum speed of 145km/h (90mph). It had servo-assisted mechanical brakes. Many versions of bodywork could be fitted on the long chassis.

This Renault proved its excellence not only in body styling and engine designing, but also in reliability and performance. On May 11, 1925, the 'teardrop' four-seater reached a speed of 172km/h (107mph) on the Montlhéry circuit. More records were to follow: in the six-hour race it averaged 157.56km/h (98mph) and a few days later it lapped the circuit for 12 hours to average 161.658km/h (100.45mph).

This car is still in perfect condition, and is in the Aalholm Automobil Museum at Nysted in Denmark.

AUSTIN SEVEN   1923

Manufactured by Austin Motor Co Ltd, Birmingham, England

In 1905 Herbert Austin (later Lord Austin of Longbridge) started designing cars in his Longbridge, Birmingham factory. He drew on his experience from working with Wolseley, a big car manufacturer.

Austin strove to meet the demand for a 'people's car', and by late 1922 he developed the Austin Seven model, known as the 'Baby Austin'.

The first Austin Seven was powered by a four-cylinder water-cooled 747 cc engine with a removable cylinder head, and a bore and stroke of 56×76.2mm, which developed 7.7kW (10.5hp) at 2400 rpm. The car had a three-speed gearbox, and was fitted with rigid axles, the front being carried on transverse semi-elliptic springs. It was fitted with four-wheel brakes — not the usual practice with small cars in 1923. The hand-brake governed the rear wheels and the foot-brake operated the front wheels. The wheels were wire-spoked, with a wheelbase of only 1.90m (6ft 3in) and a track of 1.02m (3ft 4in); the car was indeed a 'Baby'. It weighed only 360kg (794lb). The four-seater open body with a hood was fitted with wide sidescreens made of plexiglass. An electric horn was standard equipment.

The Austin Seven was made with many improvements until July 1938. An electric starter was introduced in the 1924 series. In 1925 the wheel dimensions increased, and a foot-brake operating all four wheels was introduced as late as 1931. In 1934 the gearbox became synchromesh. The last car made had the serial number 290135 on its chassis.

In 1952 the Austin Motor Co. joined Nuffield, and both merged into the British Motor Corporation.

FIAT 501 1923

Manufactured by Fiat SA, Turin, Italy

In 1919, after the end of the First World War, while the majority of European car manufacturers resumed production with tried and trusted pre-war models, Fiat amazed the world with its revolutionary 501 model. It was a vehicle of a simple design but good performance, reliable, and economical. Its bodywork started a new trend, and served as a model for European 'compact' cars. The 501, powered by a 1460 cc in-line four-cylinder engine, was designed by lawyer, Carlo Cavalli, Fiat's technical director. With it this talented and hardworking man proved his genius in mechanical designing to people who had always regarded him as only a man of the law. From 1919 to 1926 nearly 70,000 of these cars were made. The car had a four-speed gearbox, and the chassis was fitted with rigid axles supported on semi-elliptic springs. The standard model had a top speed of 70km/h (44mph). Some 2614 of the more powerful 501 S were also built, with a cruising speed as high as 100km/h (62mph).

Fiat also made the model 505, with a 2.3 litre four-cylinder engine, and the model 510 with a 3.5 litre six-cylinder engine.

In 1921 came the Super Fiat 520, of which only five were built. It had a V-12-cylinder 6805 cc engine and a maximum speed of 120km/h (130mph). The body was streamlined, but the conservatism of customers was still against such a development.

TATRA 11

Manufactured by Tatra Works Shareholding Co, Kopřivnice, Czechoslovakia

The chassis construction of the 1930s favoured independent wheel suspension. The pioneer work in this field was done by the Czechoslovak Tatra works which in 1923 announced the first production car with independent suspension, the Tatra 11. It was powered by a 1056 cc flat, air-cooled, twin-cylinder engine with valves in the cylinder head. It had bore and stroke of 82×100mm and developed 8.8kW (12hp) at 2800 rpm. The engine was fan-cooled. Ignition was provided by a Bosch magneto. The engine block, with a clutch and a gearbox, was bolted to the central tubular frame. The drive was transmitted through a dry triple-plate clutch and a four-speed gearbox to the rear axle. Semi-elliptic transverse leaf springs were fitted front and rear. Until 1926 only the rear wheels were fitted with brakes: the Tatra 12 was the first to have mechanical brakes on all four wheels. The car was supplied in various body versions. As a two-seater version it weighed 680kg (1500lb) and could reach 70km/h (44mph).

The car also made its mark in the racing field. A Tatra 11 won the first prize in the 1924 Stuttgart Solitude circuit. In the following year Tatra became the absolute winner of the longest Russian race, covering 5300 km (3290 mi) Leningrad-Moscow-Charkov-Rostov-Tbilisi, and beating 78 competitors. In the same year two Tatra 11s came first and second in their class on the Targa Florio circuit in Italy.

The Tatra 578 was the last model of this series. It was fitted with a 1256 cc flat four-cylinder air-cooled engine developing 18.4kW (25hp). The car was manufactured until 1949.

LANCIA LAMBDA 214   1923

Manufactured by Fabbrica Automobili Lancia and Cia, Turin, Italy

The Lancia Lambda was Vincenzo Lancia's masterpiece. The first prototypes were built in 1921 and exhibited at the 1922 Paris Salon. From 1923 to 1931 the Lambda was made in nine series.

The first series used a long-stroke 2120 cc engine with bore and stroke of 75×120mm. The engine's four cylinders were set at a 13° angle, arranged alternately so as to achieve the shortest possible engine length. In 1926 the seventh Lambda series was powered by a bigger engine of 2370 cc, the cylinders forming a 14° angle. The power was increased from the original 36kW (49hp) to 43.3kW (59hp). The engines of the 1928 eighth and ninth series were further bored to give 2570 cc and developed 50.7kW (69hp) at 3500 rpm. The valves were operated by an overhead camshaft fitted in the cylinder head.

Lancia replaced the then commonly-used channel section chassis by a pressed cross-member chassis frame, which dropped the weight to 780kg (1720lb). Another unusual feature was independent suspension of the front wheels using vertical coiled springs with telescopic dampers. The rigid rear axle was supported on longitudinal leaf springs and damped with shock-absorbers. With its unusually long wheelbase of 3m (10ft 2in), later stretched to 3.42m (11ft 3in), Lambda was very unconventional, but had excellent driving properties. Mechanical brakes on all wheels were fitted with brake drums with cooling ribs, and owing to the car's low weight they had excellent braking properties. A hand-brake worked on the rear wheels. The first series had a top speed of 115km/h (72mph); the last as much as 125km/h (78mph).

In the period 1923-1931 12,530 Lambdas were built. Among the characteristic features of all of them were the 5m (16ft) long body with its distinctive radiator grille, and two spare tyres.

ROLLS-ROYCE PHANTOM I   1925

Manufactured by Rolls-Royce Ltd, Derby, England

The successful Rolls-Royce 7 litre Silver Ghost, produced from 1906 to 1924, was followed in 1925 by a smaller car. It was the 3.1 litre model 20. The chassis and body were made and sold separately. The car had a four-speed gearbox, four-wheel brakes, and power steering. In 1929 the engine capacity was increased to 3.7 litres. This version, the 20/50, was manufactured as late as 1937, and it was the last Rolls which had its power specified. This almost two-tonne automobile developed 55.2kW (75hp) and had a top speed of 120km/h (75mph). From then onwards Rolls-Royce personnel, when asked about a car's power, answered tersely: 'Satisfactory'.

The good driving properties of the Silver Ghost, the 'big brother', were shared with the new Phantom. It was powered by an in-line six-cylinder 7688 cc engine of new design, with camshaft fitted in the cylinder head, and bore and stroke of 108×140mm. The estimated power was 74kW (100hp) at 3500 rpm. The car is notable for several technical advancements. A special controller was used to maintain constant, pre-selected cruising speed. Ignition advance was controlled by the oil pressure. The drive was transmitted to the rear axle via a four-speed gearbox, though the American version of the Phantom I, built in Springfield, Mass, retained left-hand steering and a three-speed gearbox until 1931. The leaf-sprung 'classical' chassis carried mechanical servo braking and hydraulic shock-absorbers. In England some 2,212 of these cars had been made by 1929.

After four years Rolls-Royce curtailed production of the Phantom I since it did not bring the success anticipated. It was replaced by the Phantom II, with the aim of establishing the company's leading position in building up-market luxury cars. In 1936 came the Phantom III, this time fitted with independent front wheel suspension, and a complicated V12-cylinder engine, adjustment of which required highly professional knowledge and expertise.

AUSTRO DAIMLER AD 6   1926

Manufactured by Austro-Daimler Gesellschaft, Wiener Neustadt, Austria

The Austrian Daimler-Motoren-Gesellschaft, which began making cars under Daimler licence in 1899, was formerly known as Maschinenfabrik Bierentz, Fischer und Co, and it made household articles. In 1905 Paul Daimler was succeeded as technical director of the company by 30-year old Ferdinand Porsche, and the company changed its name to Austro-Daimler Gesellschaft. From 1909 Austro-Daimler took part in the Prince Henry trials, regarded as the most popular event for testing reliability. Porsche proved himself to be both a brilliant engineer and driver. In 12 months he evolved a 5.9 litre four-cylinder ohc engine developing 66.2kW (90hp). The car could cruise at 146km/h (90mph). In the first event Austro-Daimler ended up with a sweeping one-two-three finish.

During the First World War Austro-Daimler became part of the Skoda concern, managed by Baron von Skoda. After the war the company introduced a stylish six-cylinder car, the AD 617, again the brainchild of Porsche. This model was made exclusively for export. The AD 617 was fitted with a 4240 cc in-line ohc engine developing 44.1kW (60hp).

In 1919 there followed the small 1.1 litre Sasha model of the Porsche series, financed by the film magnate Count Alexander Kolowrat. In this car Porsche called on his experience with the previous small Maya, named after Emile Jellinek's youngest daughter, Mercédés' sister. Originally the Sasha was intended as a production car, but postwar conditions in Austria were not favourable for implementing this programme.

In 1923 Porsche withdrew from the firm. His ideas were further developed by Karl Rabe, under whose management other AD models were built. The popular AD6 model was fitted with a 2973 cc in-line six-cylinder OHC engine developing 80.9kW (110hp). From this was derived the ADM Sport, in which the 'king of the hills' Hans Stuck won a great many hill climbs. These successes led the car to be called 'Bergmeister', the German word for 'king of the hills'.

In the early 1930s co-operation with the Austrian Puch company was started, and later the two companies merged.

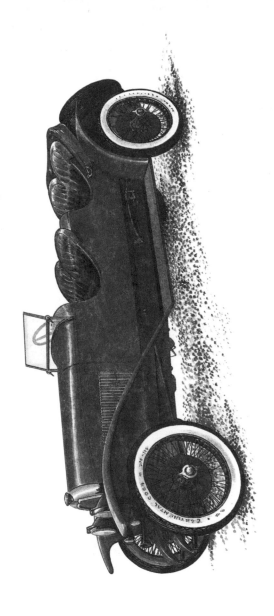

MERCEDES 630   1926

Manufactured by Daimler-Benz AG, Stuttgart-Untertürkheim, Germany

The first contacts between Daimler Motoren Gesellschaft at
Untertürkheim and Benz & Co, Rheinische Automobil und
Motorenfabrik, Mannheim were started in 1919, but it was not until
June 29, 1926, that the Daimler three-pointed star was combined with
the circular laurel wreath of Benz, and a new company, Daimler-Benz
AG, was established.

Two years before this amalgamation the 630 Mercedes model,
forerunner of the famous supercharged cars was announced. It was
also designated as 24/100/140, in which 24 indicated the taxable
horsepower, 100 the output without supercharger, and 140 the output
with supercharger. It was built by Ferdinand Porsche, who started
working for Daimler in 1923. The supercharger was developed by
Daimler's son Paul, when working as the chief designer at
Untertürkheim, but after the failure of his 2 litre sports car in
Indianapolis Paul gave up designing.

The 630 model was powered by a 6240 cc in-line six-cylinder
engine, with bore and stroke of 94×150mm and compression ratio of
4.7:1. The engine developed a maximum of 73.5kW (100hp), or 103kW
(140hp) with Root compressor, at 3000 rpm. The cylinder block,
crankcase, and pistons were fabricated from light alloy, the cylinder
liners and the valve head from cast steel. The drive was transmitted to
the rigid rear axle through a multiple disc clutch and a four-speed
gearbox. The chassis was fitted with mechanical brakes with vacuum
boosters on all wheels. This 2500kg (5500lb) seven-seater limousine,
with its 3.75m (12ft 4in) wheelbase, looked very impressive. The car
was bought by wealthy industrialists and entertainers. Soon this six-
cylinder monster tourer was followed by the 4 litre Model 400,
designated as 15/70/100. This open version was owned by President
Paul von Hindenburg of Germany.

Later on several sports cars were derived from the 630 model, such
as S, S.S. and S.S.K., which in the late 1920s and early 1930s scored
many successes in racing.

MINERVA   1927

Manufactured by Minerva Motors, Mortsel, Antwerp, Belgium

In 1900 many Belgian companies were making cars. The best-known was Minerva, which originally made bicycles and motor-cycles. The first Minerva car was made in 1900, and it was introduced by the Dutch industrialist Sylvain de Jong, founder of the company. It was a small twin-cylinder developing 4.4kW (6hp). The little Minervetta was designed specifically for the British market. It had a 636 cc single-cylinder engine developing 3.7kW (5hp). Minerva's first real success came with the six-cylinder car it announced in 1906.

In 1907 the young American Charles Y. Knight invented the sleeve-valve engine. The inlet and exhaust valves were replaced by ported cylindrical 'sleeves' that slithered between pistons and cylinders. Knight's sleeve-valve engine was very quiet and its running was very smooth. Minerva motors exhibited a Minerva powered by this very quiet six-cylinder sleeve-valve engine at the 1908 Brussels Salon. Among the first customers was Henry Ford.

After the First World War Minerva specialized in big luxury cars fitted with Knight engines. From 1921 all models had brakes fitted on the front wheels, and from 1923 the brakes had servo units.

The 1927 Minerva Torpedo was powered by a 5344 cc six-cylinder Knight engine, with bore and stroke of 90×140mm.

The original cone clutch was replaced by a disc clutch. The car had a top speed of 120km/h (75mph).

By the late 1920s Minerva got into financial difficulties. The luxury 1930 AL eight-cylinder model was the last car to be fitted with a Knight sleeve-valve engine.

In 1937 a new sensational prototype powered by a V8-cylinder engine was being discussed. The transversly mounted engine drove the front wheels. However, the car, which was to be fitted with torsion bars and automatic transmission, was never made: the company merged with the Belgian Imperia firm.

CADILLAC SERIES 314   1927

Manufactured by the Cadillac Motor Co, Detroit, Michigan, USA

In his job as a director of the Cadillac Co, Henry Leland managed to spare some time for making inventions, which included a hair-cutting appliance. He contributed to the development of car engineering by designing the automatic ignition advance, and he introduced the electric starter in mass-production cars as early as 1911.

Despite the success of mass-production Leland was not tempted by its advantages. He was resolved to manufacture the best automobiles in the world. So in 1914 he introduced an eight-cylinder model, which was to become the first production-line eight-cylinder. Soon Cadillac automobiles were the best and most expensive American cars.

One of the most luxurious Cadillacs was the 1927 model 314. The car was powered by a 5.5 litre V8-cylinder engine developing 56.8kW (80hp) at 2000 rpm. A notable feature of the engine was a flywheel with starter-generator. The model had a non-synchronized three-speed gearbox (the first synchromesh gearbox by Cadillac did not appear until 1928). The classical chassis had rigid axles front and rear supported on leaf springs. The car had mechanical brakes fitted to all wheels, and the rear had duplex band and shoe brakes. The Cadillac 314, weighing 2150kg (4740lb), would do 130km/h (80mph). Apart from the normal headlights the car carried additional lamps which changed direction according to the position of the front wheels. Reversing lights came on when reverse gear was engaged. Other lavish equipment included a silver-plated instrument panel, upholstery in two kinds of red leather, interior lights with door contact illuminating the floor area, and an air compressor for pumping up the tyres.

Several tens of thousands of Cadillacs were manufactured each year, and their price was four times that of an average American car.

FRANKLIN   1927

Manufactured by Franklin Automobile Co, Syracuse, New York, USA

The Franklin company was established by Herbert Franklin in Syracuse, N Y in 1901. John Wilkinson, designer of these successful automobiles, only used air-cooled engines in his cars: in his opinion, water-cooling was a useless complication.

A car fitted with an air-cooled engine was introduced by Franklin as early as 1902. Two years later this car was to break the then record of 61 days in the San Francisco-New York trials. The 1909 Franklin model performed a similar drive in 1976, this time from Istanbul to San Francisco. The car had a 2 litre in-line, four-cylinder engine which developed 10.3kW (14hp). Cooling was fan-assisted, the fan being mounted in the flywheel. The engine had magneto ignition. The Franklin was notable for its wooden chassis frame and full-elliptic sprung rigid axles front and rear. A feature was a dummy radiator — fitted for conservative customers only. The drive was transmitted via a three-speed gearbox to the rear axle, to which was fitted an outer band brake. The car weighed 760kg (1675lb). The company specified the car's maximum speed as 75km/h (47mph).

In the 1920s Franklin built a new 12-cylinder model, assisted by designer Glen Shoemaker. The four-stroke, air-cooled OHV engine had a capacity of 6585 cc. Fitted with a two-speed gearbox, the car reached a maximum speed of 150km/h (93mph). The rigid axles were suspended on semi-elliptic springs. This almost three-tonne 'tank' was quiet unlike earlier Franklin models, and was heavy on fuel.

In the 1930s the company developed a new 12-cylinder model, Series 17, the last car it made. Financial problems put an end to production in 1933.

CHEVROLET CAPITOL 1927

Manufactured by Chevrolet Motor Co, Detroit, Michigan, USA

Louis Chevrolet, who successfully raced in Buick cars, decided to establish a company to make cars of his own design. So in 1911 the Chevrolet Motor Co. was founded in Detroit, Michigan. A year later the company produced its first car.

Louis Chevrolet did not stay long with his company. In 1917 he sold it to William Crapo Durand, founder of General Motors, and Chevrolet joined Buick, Oldsmobile, Cadillac, and Oakland in G M.

In 1922 William Knudsen, a Dane by birth, was appointed director of the Chevrolet works. Knudsen, a former director at Henry Ford's, introduced an efficient assembly-line. Under his guidance, Chevrolet soon started producing cars which cost the same as those made by Ford, but were even better and bigger. This probably led to the curtailment of production of Ford's successful Model T, and Chevrolet became the leader in American car production.

The Chevrolet Capitol was among the successful types of this period. The car had a 2760 cc four-cylinder in-line engine, air-cooled and OHV, which developed 19.1kW (26hp) at 1800 rpm. The drive was transmitted via a three-speed gearbox to the rear wheels. The oblong frame had rigid axles supported on longitudinal leaf springs. The Capitol was not fitted with brakes on the front wheels since in the company's opinion they were unnecessary for a car weighing only 910kg (2000lb). With a two-door bodywork, the Capitol had a top speed of 80km/h (50mph).

The firm introduced front-wheel brakes in 1928, because the rapidly increasing traffic in American cities demanded four-wheel braking.

VOLVO ÖV 4   1927

Manufactured by AB Volvo Car Division, Göteborg, Sweden

Two young men, businessman Assar Gabrielsson and design engineer Gustav Larson, were responsible for the start of Volvo car production. In 1927, the year Henry Ford stopped making his successful Model T, the first production Volvo left the assembly line in Göteborg. An elegant five-seater, it was designated as ÖV 4, but became more popular under its nickname 'Jakob'.

Jakob was powered by a 1944 cc air-cooled four-cylinder engine, developing 20.7kW (28hp) with a maximum speed of 60km/h (37mph). The car had a steel-covered wooden cabriolet body. Even though the rugged chassis was designed for the rough Scandinavian roads, the open body was not exactly compatible with the Swedish climate. During the car's production life only some 205 were built. Later the company produced a closed PV 4 version. This time commercial success came quickly, and Volvo started exporting cars to Finland, Norway, and Denmark.

The first six-cylinder Volvo was announced in 1929, with a water-cooled in-line engine developing 40kW (55hp), hydraulic brakes, and a synchromesh gearbox. The car had a top speed of 110km/h (68mph). The first streamlined car was the Carioca, introduced in 1935. Its six-cylinder engine developed as much as 62kW (84hp). Independent front wheel suspension guaranteed comfort and good driving. But by 1938 only 500 cars had been manufactured because of the high price.

A sensation of the 1944 Stockholm Car Exhibition was the new PV 444 model. The car had a body-shell construction and an economical four-cylinder engine developing 30kW (40hp). The car was also equipped with a new safety feature, a laminated front windscreen. The car was awarded a first prize for its smart body design at a show in Heidelberg. The car design stayed basically unchanged until 1965.

In 1959 Volvo was the first company in the world to equip its production cars with safety belts. The modern Volvos are well known for exceptional reliability and safety features.

PRAGA GRAND   1927

Manufactured by Českomoravská Kolben-Daněk as, Prague, Czechoslovakia

Praga, the Latin form of Prague, was adopted as the name for the cars built at the Prague automobile factory from as early as 1909.

In 1912 a new passenger car, the Grand, was built there, and it was the most powerful model of the Praga series. Three of the earliest Grands were entered for the 2700 km (1680 mi) Alpine Trial, which they won, outstripping even Rolls-Royce. The Praga Grand of the first series was powered by a 3824 cc water-cooled four-cylinder engine which developed 33.1kW (45hp). After a second victory by Praga cars in the next Alpine Trial, the Hungarian carriage works in Rába applied for a licence to make and sell those cars in Hungary.

In 1927 the Czech company extended its production programme by two in-line six-cylinders, Alfa and Mignon, and the Grand model was fitted with a 3384 cc in-line eight-cylinder side-valve engine, with bore and stroke of 70×110mm. The engine was fitted with two horizontal Zenith carburettors, and developed 44.1kW (60hp). The rigid axles, suspended on semi-elliptic springs, from an ordinary chassis, were damped by Delco-Rémy double-acting liquid shock-absorbers. A servo-unit increased the efficiency of the mechanical brakes on all four wheels. The car weighed 1900kg (4190lb) and achieved a maximum speed of 100km/h (62mph). Various kinds of bodies were fitted to the chassis, such as the convertible type built under licence from Kellner et Fils, an outstanding Paris bodymaker, or closed six- to seven-seaters, the so-called *conduites intérieures* (interior drives).

The car's equipment could be varied to suit the customer's requirements. The most luxurious models were fitted with spoke-wheels, a driver's telephone, a stick-holder, an air-compressor for pumping up tyres, illumination of the footboard when opening the door, and automatic return of the direction indicators. The interior was richly decorated with inlayed woodwork.

Later the eight-cylinder engine was re-bored to 80mm, thus increasing the capacity to 4429 cc, and the power to develop 66.2kW (90hp) at 3000 rpm. Of the total of 1200 cars produced the last left the factory in 1934.

BMW DIXI   1928

Manufactured by Dixi-Werke, Eisenach, Germany

The Eisenach car factory was established in 1896. The main shareholder was Heinrich Eberhardt, nicknamed in Germany the 'Second Cannon King'.

The company's first vehicle was shown at the Düsseldorf Automobile Exhibition in 1898, but without any commercial success. So Eisenach bought a licence from Décauville in 1898 and started manufacturing the well-tried Voiturettes under the name of Wartburg-Motorwagen. Eberhardt withdrew from Eisenach Fahrzeugfabrik in 1904, his departure also ending the French licence. A new wave in the company's technical development came with the arrival of designer Willy Seck, who had been working with the Scheibler company in Aachen.

The Dixi-Werke had a boom period in the early 1920s. In those days, most German motor companies were wishfully thinking of a small yet powerful production car. Dixi abandoned an expensive and time-consuming development programme, and decided to obtain a licence from the Austin Motor Co. of Birmingham, which had been manufacturing the Austin Seven since 1922. This, the Baby Austin, was the most successful small British car. Early in 1928 this car was introduced to the German public as the Dixi 3/15. Mass-production commenced immediately after this début. The Dixi 3/15 had a quiet 748 cc water-cooled four-cylinder engine. With a power of 11kW (15hp) the car developed a maximum speed of 80km/h (50mph). A hand-brake worked on the front wheels, and a pedal-brake on the rear wheels. In the Eisenach version, battery ignition replaced Austin's magneto ignition. Initially the automobile was manufactured in an open version with a hood. Later it appeared in a limousine version, too.

In 1928 Dixi was bought by BMW. Between then and 1932 a total of 25,365 of what was then called the BMW-Dixi were manufactured.

ISOTTA-FRASCHINI TIPO 8A   1929

Manufactured by Fabbrica Automobili Isotta-Fraschini, Milan, Italy

Rolls-Royce, Hispano-Suiza, and Isotta-Fraschini represented the most luxurious cars available in the 1920s. Isotta-Fraschini, making prestige high-performance automobiles powered by large-capacity engines, was a pioneer of four-wheel brakes, and mass-production of eight-cylinder in-line engines.

The company started the era of eight-cylinder engines with its 1919 model Tipo 8, replaced in 1924 by the improved Tipo 8A. The original 7300 cc engine had 95mm bore and 130mm stroke. The engine block was a one-piece aluminium casting, like that of the company's aircraft engines. The pistons were also made of aluminium alloy. Two Zenith carburettors were fitted. The ten-bearing crankshaft was damped by a torsional-vibration damper. The engine developed from 81 to 88kW (110 to 120hp) at 2400 rpm. The drive was transmitted via a propeller shaft and a multiple-disc clutch through a three-speed gearbox to the rear axle. Vacuum-assisted brakes on all four wheels were standard equipment. The hand-brake operated on all wheels, too. The chassis, with rigid axles, had semi-elliptic springs with friction dampers. The chassis alone weighed 1500kg (3000lb), and was fitted with a body made by a bodymaker chosen by the customer. The silent film star Rudolf Valentino owned an Isotta-Fraschini fitted with an American Fleetwood body.

The coachwork of the model shown here was made by the Milanese bodymaker Cesare Sala. From 1928 Isotta-Fraschini also made complete cars.

In the late 1920s Isotta-Fraschini embarked on the production of its fastest and most luxurious automobiles, introducing the Tipo 8ASS to the market. Its engine, with a high degree of compression, bigger valves, and twin-carburettors developed 100 to 110kW (135 to 150hp). In third gear the car could accelerate smoothly from 8km/h to 180km/h (5-112mph).

MERCEDES-BENZ SS   1929

Manufactured by Daimler-Benz AG, Stuttgart-Untertürkheim, Germany

After Gottlieb Daimler's son Paul retired from his post of chief designer at Untertürkheim, where he had been since 1907, Ferdinand Porsche was the new name in the Mercedes design department. Porsche designed 2 litre eight-cylinder engines developing 95.53kW (130hp), or 110.2kW (150hp) with supercharger, which were used in the racing cars. At the same time he produced six-cylinder engines designed for production cars. These cars were the 400 fitted with a 4 litre engine and developing 51.48kW (70hp) or 73.47kW (100hp) with a supercharger, and the 630 with a 6.3 litre engine developing 73.47kW (100hp) or 102.26kW (140hp) respectively.

In 1926 Daimler and Benz merged as Daimler-Benz AG. In 1927 the new firm responded to the modern designing trends by announcing 2500kg (5500lb) cars with large wheels, and a new type, 630 K. 'K' stood for short wheelbase (Kurz). The 630 K was followed by the 680 S, on which successful racing cars were based owing to the car's light chassis. The engine's capacity was steadily increased and the chassis weight dropped from 1500 to 1270kg (3300-2800lb). Then the 710 SS with a 7065 cc engine was announced. With a bore and stroke of 100×150mm it could develop 124kW (170hp) at 2900 rpm, or 150.61kW (225hp) at 3300 rpm in the supercharged version. The engine was of an advanced design: the engine block, the cranckcase, the cylinder heads, and pistons were made of light alloys. The liners and the cylinder head were cast steel, the crankshaft was of chrome-nickel steel. The engine was sealed with a gasket only, placed under the cylinder head. This car scored its first win in the 1927 Nürburgring race, where Mercedes were placed first, second, third and fifth.

In 1928 Ferdinand Porsche left the company. His successor Hans Nibel, also an outstanding engineer, strongly influenced further development of the factory.

From 1929 onwards the short version, designated SSK, was mostly built for racing, and the SS was fitted with passenger bodies. Over the years 1928-1934 a total of 300 of the S, SS, SSK, and SSKL models were built.

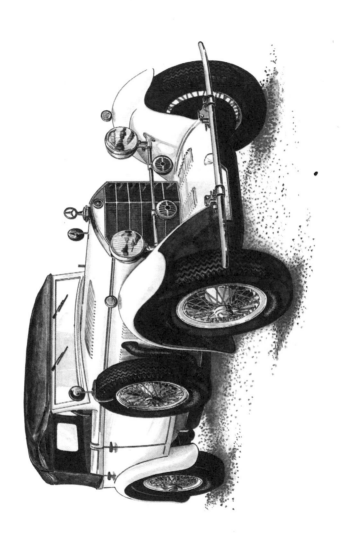

ALFA ROMEO 6 C 1750 GRAN SPORT   1930

Manufactured by SA Alfa Romeo, Milan, Italy

The name of Alfa Romeo is synonymous with the great sporting successes this firm has had since 1923, when it embarked on a systematic racing programme. Alfa Romeo made its reputation with its excellent P2 racers. Vittorio Jano, the chief designer of Alfa Romeo, was inspired by the success of the P2, and began a new series of high-performance sports cars. The first six-cylinder engines, with one camshaft mounted in the cylinder head, had a capacity of 1.5 litres. Thanks to the engine power of 441.1kW (60hp) at 4500 rpm, the cars reached a speed of 120km/h (75mph).

The most notable of this series was undoubtedly the six-cylinder Gran Sport, powered by a 1752 cc in-line water-cooled engine of 65mm bore and 88mm stroke. The excellent craftsmanship of this engine even surpassed the sophisticated mechanisms of Bugatti. Two camshafts in the cylinder head were driven by a vertical bevel drive shaft. When fitted with a Roots supercharger the engine developed 62kW (84hp) at 4500 rpm. The drive was transmitted to the rear rigid axle via a dry multiple-disc clutch. The chassis, made of the best materials, had both rigid axles supported on semi-elliptic leaf springs. The simple, yet elegant body with a characteristic high footboard, was designed by the bodymaker Zagato. The fuel tank, two batteries, and a large luggage compartment filled the massive rear part of the body. The car had a top speed of 145km/h (90mph).

The last series, the 6 C 1750 Gran Sport, had a 77.2kW (105hp) engine, giving a top speed of 170km/h (106mph) and a 10-second acceleration from 0 to 100km/h (62mph).

A total of 320 of this famous model were built by 1934. From 1965 the Zagato body-workshop made copies of the Gran Sport, with the traditional body mounted on a contemporary chassis.

BUGATTI 35 B   1930

Manufactured by E. Bugatti, Molsheim, France

A new Bugatti, type 35, the development of which had begun as early as the winter of 1923, appeared at the French Grand Prix in 1924. The car was fitted with an eight-cylinder 2 litre engine with one camshaft in the cylinder head, and stroke and bore of 88×60mm, designed for the earlier type 30 in 1922.

The eight-cylinder engine had two cast-iron blocks of four cylinders each. Each cylinder was fitted with two inlet valves and one exhaust valve. The engine had only a small radiator, and ran without a fan even in the Targa Florio hill climb. The oil-tank was modified to be an oil-cooler through which led 13 copper tubes conducting the cooling air flow. The most expensive part of the car was a composite nine-piece camshaft, the price of which was equivalent to the cost of the whole chassis of a Bugatti 40 in 1927.

The greatest asset of these cars was the excellent chassis, with perfect track keeping and smooth steering. A feature was the rigid axle suspension on reversely mounted quarter-elliptic springs. The hollow one-piece forged front axle of circular cross-section was a masterpiece of smithery: it was successively turned, bent, tempered, and polished. The mechanical brakes were fitted with an automatic adjustment to allow for uneven wear. The brake drums and brake shoes were cooled by the fan effect of the wheels. The wood-inlayed four-spoke steering wheel, with a diameter of 424mm (17in), moved the front wheels completely at one turn. The aluminium body was hand made.

From the viewpoint of body-styling the cars were very elegant. Bugatti was very particular about the surface finish of all parts, the simple form of which, together with the beauty of their engineering, is still admired.

A total of 200 type 35 were built. This number included the 35 A with the composite camshaft; 35 B with a 2661 cc engine; and a supercharged type 35 C. The designation 35 T appeared after the brilliant victory of Bartolomeo Constantini in the 1926 Targa Florio circuit in Sicily. The Bugatti 35 is generally considered to be Ettore Bugatti's finest car, even though he designed many notable cars afterwards.

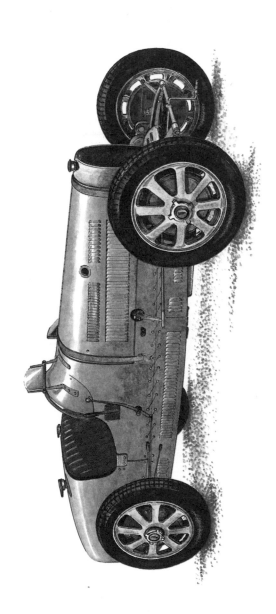

BENTLEY 4.5 LITRE   1931

Manufactured by Bentley Motors Ltd, Derby, England

Walter Owen Bentley was among the greatest automobile designers of his time. His first invention should have secured him financially for life: it was an engine with aluminium pistons, which facilitated production of the best aircraft engines during the First World War. But he was in uniform, and Bentley's invention was 'appreciated' by promotion to the rank of lieutenant. After the war he rented a small workshop and started building cars. The first 1919 prototype had a 3 litre four cylinder engine. The cylinders were fitted with duplex plugs and exhaust and inlet valves.

Volume production commenced in 1921. Right from the beginning this 3 litre model became a hit of the motor industry. The Bentley factory gave a five-year guarantee on the car. In contrast to Rolls-Royce cars, this model was not designed to be chauffeur-driven, since driving a Bentley car implied sporting ambitions.

The cars sold well, and Bentley increased production to eight cars in a week. The 3 litre type with the Red Label, the most famous model, was the prototype from which many other models were derived, among them the Green Label, with a shorter chassis, and the more powerful Blue Label. Some 500 cars survive out of the 1600 manufactured. Based on the popular 3 litre Speed Six, a new type was developed, the engine capacity being increased to 4398 cc, with 100mm bore and 140mm stroke.

In 1926 a new 6.5 litre Big Six was announced, with a six-cylinder engine whose bore and stroke dimensions of 100×140mm were identical to those of the Hispano-Suiza engine.

The trend towards large capacity engines was continued in the next model. This time it was an 8 litre six-cylinder. W. O. Bentley did not try to build comfortable automobiles. His policy was based on large, powerful, and solidly elegant cars.

In spite of the popularity of his models, the company suffered from financial difficulties. The Great Depression ruined Bentley. Besides his factory he lost his own property, including his private Bentley car. The debts were paid off by Rolls-Royce, which also employed Bentley — but only to demonstrate new models to customers.

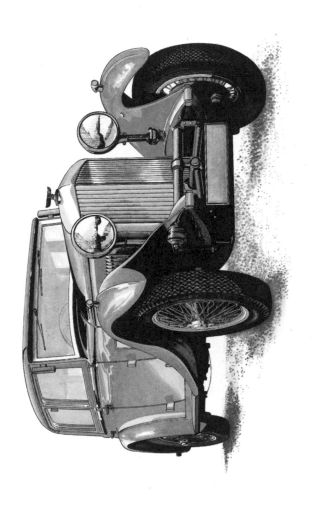

BENTLEY LE MANS   1931

Manufactured by Bentley Motors Ltd, Derby, England

W. O. Bentley's greatest passion was car racing. The famous Oulton Park Rally offered a good opportunity for seeing 200 Bentley cars, almost the only entrants in the event.

In 1923 several automobile fans decided to organize a 24-hour race. The French town of Le Mans was chosen for the venue. In the first year a Bentley driven by a private owner came fourth. A year later the factory car won the race and from 1927 to 1930 Bentleys scored victories in this event. It seemed as if the cars with the winged 'B' on the radiator grille were failure-proof. While the competing cars took turns in the pits with engine trouble the Bentleys carried on. Famous driving teams such as J. D. Benjafield, S. C. H. Davis, Woolf Barnato-Bernard Rubin, Barnato-Henry Birkin and Barnato-Glen Kidston were behind the wheel of Bentleys from 1927 until 1930. In 1929 and 1930 the 6.5 litre cars contributed to the majority of victories. Ettore Bugatti called them 'the fastest trucks in the world'. With the engine developing almost 147kW (200hp) they had a top speed of 180km/h (112mph).

But these years of success came to an abrupt end. A new 8 litre model was practically unsaleable. The Depression period was not favourable for selling luxurious automobiles. Bentley left his new employers, Rolls-Royce, and joined the rival Lagonda company, where he built a 12-cylinder giant called Lagonda-Bentley. But this was the last time that the name of this outstanding designer appeared independently.

BUGATTI 41 ROYALE, COUPÉ DE VILLE 1931

Manufactured by Ettore Bugatti, Molsheim, France

The designer of this 'royal' car, Ettore Bugatti, had long been thinking of building a large, powerful, quiet and fast luxurious automobile of elegant form. He believed that he could create a masterpiece. Because of racing successes his financial situation was good enough to make his grand plan possible. It is said that the final stimulas came from an English lady, who remarked that while Bugatti built the fastest cars, when it came to the best, one had to turn to Rolls-Royce.

Originally Bugatti had planned to manufacture some 25 Royales fitted with 15 litre engines. However, for various reasons only seven cars were made. The prototype appeared in June 1928, after four years' development. With an engine capacity of 14,726 cc and a 4.57m (15ft) wheelbase, it was the sensation of the year. The models that followed had engines of 12,763 cc and a wheelbase shortened to 4.30m (14ft 2in).

The eight-cylinder engine was derived from a 16-cylinder Bugatti aircraft engine used during the First World War. It was almost 1.5m (5ft) long and weighed 380kg (840lb). The crankshaft alone weighed 175.5kg (303lb). The OHC engine developed 220kW (300hp) at 1700 rpm. First gear was engaged only when starting up the car and when tackling extremely steep gradients. Owing to the unusual adaptability of the engine, second gear could be engaged from standstill up to a speed of 150km/h (93mph). The car's maximum speed was approximately 200km/h (125mph), but varied according to the bodywork.

It is really hard to imagine a 6.5m (21ft 4in) long passenger car with a 2m (21ft 4in) long passenger car with a 2m (6ft 6in) long bonnet and tyres of 970mm (38in) diameter. Especially noteworthy was the single-piece front axle fabricated from stainless steel, with a hollow central section. Both ends of the axle are bored to accomodate wedged leaf springs.

Only seven Bugatti Royale engines were mounted in cars, the rest were fitted in special express trains, the so-called Autorails. The 'Presidential' autorail, with four Royales, achieved a top speed of 196km/h (122mph).

DUESENBERG J   1931

Manufactured by the Duesenberg Motor Co, Indianapolis, Indiana, USA

When the Duesenberg brothers, Fred and August, descendants of German immigrants, began to manufacture cars in 1919, neither would have thought that their automobiles would become the most admired American cars of the 1930s.

The cars manufactured in the Indianapolis factory were hand-built, including the body, and during the firm's existence no more than 650 sports and touring models were made.

The J series Duesenberg had an in-line, liquid-cooled, four-valve, eight-cylinder OHC engine of 6882 cc, which at 4200 rpm and a compression ratio of 5.2 developed 195kW (265hp). It had a Schebler carburettor and a dynamo-battery ignition system. The massive chassis was centrally lubricated. The rigid axles were suspended on semi-elliptic springs with Watson friction dampers. The hydraulic brakes were boosted to cope with the car's total weight of 2100kg (4630lb) and a top speed of 190km/h (118mph). In spite of its weight, the car could accelerate from 0 to 160km/h (0-99mph) in 21 seconds.

A notable feature was the dashboard. Apart from the usual instruments it also contained an altimeter, a barometer, a tyre air-pressure indicator, and an oil-change indicator which lit up after every 1130 km (700 mi). Other instruments showed the radiator water level and indicated low brake fluid.

The best bodymakers, among them Murphy, Brunn, Le Baron, and Derham, were eager to style Duesenberg cars. The car's interior was decorated with leather or brocade, and could be fitted with special lighting, a telephone, or a bar.

Owing to the very high price of the car only kings, maharajahs, and film-stars could afford it. The car was nicknamed the 'Cooper' after one of its early owners, the actor Gary Cooper.

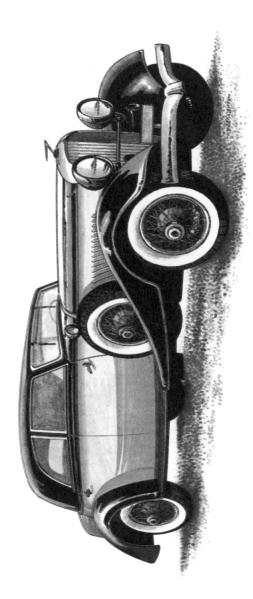

CHRYSLER 1931

Manufactured by Chrysler Corporation, Detroit, USA

In contrast to the other founders of American motor companies, Walter Chrysler was one of the greatest industrialists of his time, thanks to his ambition and initiative.

He started work as a railway mechanic, and by the age of 40 succeeded to the post of president of General Motors. Unfortunately, his ideas differed from the interests of William Crapo Durand, founder of G M, and Chrysler solved the dispute by leaving the company.

In 1924 he and three young engineers, Fred Zeder, Owen Skelton, and Carl Breer, established a new independent motor company. The products of the Chrysler Corporation soon earned a reputation for high quality. In 1925 a car was produced with a six-cylinder side-valve engine developing 50kW (68hp) at 3800 rpm. Lockheed hydraulic brakes were fitted on all four wheels.

The model 50 was introduced in 1927. The coupé, with a two-seater body, and detachable wooden wheels, had a 2790 cc in-line four-cylinder engine with thermo-syphon cooling, an electric starter, and a disc-clutch. The windscreen wipers, an electric horn, a rear-view mirror, and even an anti-theft device, were standard equipment.

After the Dodge brothers died, Chrysler bought the Dodge Motor Co, and became the third biggest American can manufacturer after General Motors and Ford.

The 1931 model CD had a 4396 cc in-line eight-cylinder engine, with a fuel pump. Hydraulic brakes, a radiator with a thermostat, and a four-speed gearbox were standard equipment.

One of the most discussed models was the Airflow, the name being inspired by the car's streamlined body. The public were rather cool, and in four years only 30,000 of the cars were purchased.

Walter Chrysler died in 1940, but the trademark he established still ranks among the giants.

MERCEDES-BENZ SSK 1931

Manufactured by Daimler-Benz AG, Stuttgart-Untertürkheim, Germany

The Daimler company introduced its first supercharged car at the Berlin Automobile Exhibition as early as 1921. It was the 6/25/40. The long-stroke engine with bore and stroke of 68×108mm gave a capacity of 1570 cc. The camshaft was fitted in the cylinder head. The Roots supercharger was brought into operation by a special clutch when the accelerator pedal was depressed smartly.

The SSK appeared on the market in 1929. Initially it was fitted with the same engine as the SS, with a capacity of 7065 cc and bore and stroke of 100×150mm. The production versions developed 125kW (170hp) at 2900 rpm or 166kW (225hp) at 3300 rpm respectively.

At that time the production cars could be entered for Grand Prix competitions. The SSK started its series of victories in a hill climb. For this model the wheelbase of the SS chassis was shortened from 3.4m (11ft 2in) to 2930mm (9ft 8in). The shorter version was designated SSK, the abbreviation standing for Super Sport Kurz (Super Sports Short). The performance of this sports and racing car was increased. The engine, with the same capacity, was rated at 133kW (180hp) at 2900 rpm or at 184kW (250hp) at 3300 rpm with a supercharger. The car could reach 200km/h (125mph). Various body types, among them roadsters, cabriolets, tourers and racers, were fitted to the chassis.

The racing versions called for the lowest weight possible. Therefore a light Mercedes version was built, the SSKL. The simplest way to cut down the weight was to drill holes in the frame. Only 42 of the SSKL and SSK cars were made.

In 1930 Hans Nibel, who designed these successful models, again increased the output of his engines to 200kW (300hp) at 3400 rpm with a supercharger. The era of the Mercedes racers had started. There were only a few drivers capable of handling these giants, which did not have power steering. The difficult gear shifting and insensitive brakes on the one hand, and the responsive supercharger on the other, gave the drivers a hard time. Among those who had mastered these cars were Rudolf Caracciola, Manfred von Brauchitsch, and Hans Stuck.

PIERCE-ARROW 41   1931

Manufactured by the Pierce-Arrow Motor Car Co, Buffalo, New York, USA

Between 1928 and 1933 Pierce-Arrow was an independent trademark within the Studebaker company, into which it was incorporated due to its financial difficulties.

During the slump in the American motor industry the Studebaker company moved its factories to Canada, but even this measure could not save the company for long, and in 1966 the firm ceased to build cars.

Originally the Studebaker family built the famous pioneer wagons for the first conquerors of the West. The famous 1850 Conestoga model, called 'the Prairie Schooner', was supplied to the Union during the Civil War by Studebaker and according to General Ulysses S. Grant, the Union commander, they were a decisive factor in the war.

One of the remarkable Pierce-Arrow cars, with its characteristic emblem of an archer on the radiator grille, was the 1931 Pierce-Arrow 41. This car was fitted with an in-line eight-cylinder engine hidden under an almost 1.5m (5ft) long bonnet. The water-cooled side-valve 6360cc engine, with bore and stroke of 89×127mm, developed 97kW (132hp). Power was transmitted via a three-speed gearbox. The fuel-mixture was provided by a Stromberg carburettor. The car had an oblong chassis frame. Both the front and the rear axles were suspended on semi-elliptic leaf springs, whose 1.5m (5ft) length guaranteed the travelling comfort required in this luxury class of car. The 1350kg (2980lb) chassis, carried bodies by various bodymakers. The car had a top speed of 140km/h (87mph).

ALVIS   1932

Manufactured by the Alvis Car and Engineering Co Ltd, Coventry, England

The Alvis trademark was established in 1920 when Thomas George John took over the Holley Brothers Co. Ltd. producing light alloy pistons, and began the manufacture of motorcycles and cars. His first car was a four-cylinder 1.4 litre car, followed by bigger types with engine volumes increased to 4.6 litres.

Alvis specialized in front-wheel drive. The company entered for sporting events from the very beginning. Its first racing car was fitted with a four-cylinder 1.5 litre supercharged engine which developed 74kW (100hp). The vehicle, weighing as little as 475kg (1050lb), was exceptionally fast and maintained an average speed of 169km/h (105mph) at Brooklands. The car was remarkable for its unusually long bonnet, covering a four-speed gearbox which was placed in front of the engine. Behind the gearbox was the front axle differential. Although the company was a regular competitor at Brooklands it could not make its mark against such cars as Bugatti, Delage or Talbot-Darracq. After its 1927 racing failure the company decided to withdraw from building Grand Prix racers and devoted its production to tourers and sports cars. During that period the 1.5 litre Alvis was built, fitted with a 1482 cc four-cylinder engine with the camshaft in the cylinder head. The car developed 37kW (50hp) without a supercharger, or 55kW (75hp) when supercharged. It had independent suspension for all four wheels. Owing to financial difficulties the firm gave up making front-wheel drive cars in 1929.

From among the classical types with rear-axle drive the 1932 model Speed Twenty, successful in many sporting events, should be mentioned. The name of the company was changed to Alvis Ltd. in 1936. The firm, which also made aircraft engines, ceased to exist in 1967.

BUGATTI 50 T   1932

Manufactured by Automobiles Ettore Bugatti, Molsheim, France

In the late 1920s supercharged cars gained leading positions in competitive motoring. None of the companies winning Grand Prix entered for the races without a supercharged engine, whether it was Alfa-Romeo, Maserati, Delage, Talbot, or Bugatti.

Ettore Bugatti accepted supercharged engines in 1926, although he had resented this invention at first, and even in 1924, after a series of victories by his model 35, he proclaimed that his cars needed no superchargers in order to win.

As Bugatti's models were sold privately in versions almost identical to those of the racers, the supercharged cars became known to the public at large.

In 1930 Bugatti put a new supercharged car, Type 50, on the market. The 4972 cc engine had two camshafts, located in the cylinder head, and bore and stroke of 86×107mm. Its eight-cylinders, with nine-bearing crankshaft, had a better-designed combustion area than that of earlier engines of identical capacity, and could develop as much as 166.5kW (225hp) at 4000 rpm. The mixture was provided by two Schebler carburettors, and supercharging by a Roots compressor. The rear rigid axle, suspended on quarter-elliptic springs, carried a three-speed gearbox. The mechanical brakes operated on all four wheels. The aluminium-alloy cast wheels, specially designed by Bugatti, were blade-shaped in order to cool the brake drums. The 1700kg (3750lb) car had a top speed of 185km/h (115mph).

In 1932 a tourer version, the Bugatti 50 T appeared, fitted with a less powerful 147kW (200hp) engine. It had a 3.5m (11ft 6in) wheelbase, longer than the original 3.1m (10ft 2in). The car reached a speed of 175km/h (109mph). This sports-tourer model was noteworthy for its splendid coupé coachwork with sharply sloping windscreen. Altogether 100 of these cars were built between 1930 and 1934.

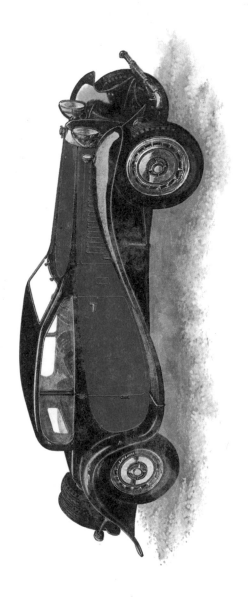

CORD L 29   1932

Manufactured by Auburn Automobile Co, Auburn, Indiana, USA

Erret Lobban Cord was a very successful businessman. At the age of
35 he became president of the giant holding company which
incorporated the Auburn-Cord and Duesenberg trademarks. Cord
realized that he had to offer something exceptional in the face of
intense competition. So he turned to the Indianapolis racing-car
designers Henry Miller and Cornelius W. van Ranst to develop a front
wheel-drive tourer. The result was the Cord L 29, with a body like a
Duesenberg. The main difference between the two makes was the
front-wheel drive.

The car was powered by a 4934 cc in-line eight-cylinder engine
developing 92kW (125hp) at 3300 rpm. Engines were supplied with
the compression ratios of 5.25 or 6.5 to 1. There was a five-bearing,
crankshaft and the air-fuel mixture was provided by a duplex Schebler
carburettor. The front-mounted gearbox was controlled by a lever
located on the instrument panel.

The instrument panel alone was a notable feature of the car. It had a
great number of gauges and control lights indicating among other
things, water temperature, oil pressure, oil level, ignition, and the inlet
air temperature. The chassis was suspended on quarter-elliptic leaf
springs in the front and semi-elliptic at the rear. Large drum brakes,
with a diameter of 300mm (11½in) in front and 381mm (15in) at the
rear provided for adequate braking.

Driving the Cord felt different from driving other cars of the 1930s.
The car was 250mm (10in) lower to the ground than that of its
contemporaries and the front-drive together with the large-diameter
tyres created a feeling of great stability. This feature made the car very
popular as a getaway vehicle for gangster drivers.

However, the car did not sell well, because of its high price and the
New York Stock Exchange slump. Only 5000 were made between
1930 and 1932.

FORD A   1927

Manufactured by Ford Motor Company, Dearborn, Michigan, USA

In 1927, the whole motoring world was shocked: Henry Ford closed down car production in all his factories. Ford's successful Model T was gone forever. The 'Tin Lizzie' was intended to be a car that would never become outmoded and could be modernized and updated with spare parts. But after a production life of 19 years, it had to be dropped. The ladies were partly to be blamed for this, since they refused to crank up the engine with the starting handle, but the main reason was that the car *had* become obsolete. But Ford shut down only to try his luck with an entirely new model, which emerged six months later. To build it, Ford had to modify or replace 45,000 single-purpose machines.

The A model appeared at the end of 1927. It was fitted with a 3285 cc four-cylinder in-line side-valve engine, developing 29.4kW (40hp) at 2200 rpm. The drive was transmitted via a disc clutch and a three-speed gearbox to the rear axle. The chassis was fitted with rigid axles suspended on transverse semi-elliptic springs. The wire-spoke wheels had mechanical brakes. The 1075kg (2370lb) limousine had a top speed of 100km/h (62mph). The new model was produced in accordance with the well-tried Ford method: 4000 in the first year of production, 800,000 in the second year, and finally 1,800,000 a year.

Ford did not neglect export. He avoided high import duties by establishing factories in England and Germany. In Cologne, he laid the foundation stone of the most advanced European car factory of the 1930s. There he built a small Continental 2 litre car developing 20.6kW (28hp) at 2200 rpm.

But competition was merciless in the 1930s. When Ford brought out his four-cylinder model A, his rivals at General Motors Corporation introduced a comfortable six-cylinder Chevrolet, which did not cost a dollar more than the A model. As a result production of the Model A came to an end within five years.

AERO 662 1933

Manufactured by Aero-Praha, Prague, Czechoslovakia

The Aero factory in Prague built and repaired aircraft. Then came a slump in aircraft sales, and the company searched for new possibilities. In 1925 the factory obtained a licence to build car bodies, and Dr. Kabeš, the factory's owner, also concluded contracts to provide coachwork for foreign car makers.

The early Aero cars were based on a Czech car, the Enka, produced by the Košař company until 1928. The first car, the Aero 500, had a two-stroke single-cylinder 499 cc engine which developed 7.3kW (10hp) at 2700 rpm.

In 1931, the Aero was fitted with a two-stroke twin-cylinder 662 cc engine with bore and stroke of 75×75mm. The model was designated '662' in reference to the engine's capacity. The engine had thermo-syphon water cooling. The dynamo-battery ignition was controlled by two crankshaft cams and its advance could be adjusted for starting and city traffic, or for the open road. The engine was fitted with an American sleeve-valve Amal carburettor. The drive was transmitted via a cone clutch to a three-speed gearbox located on the rear axle. Both rigid axles were suspended on quarter-elliptic springs, with friction dampers on the front axle.

Aero cars were manufactured in different versions. The basic type was a two-seater with a roadster body and a rumble seat in the luggage space. The company also produced four-seaters with roadster or limousine coachwork, and closed or open vans. The car version, with wire-spoke wheels and front wheel brakes, had a top speed of 90km/h (56mph). The car could be supplied with a differential on request.

After 1934 the design of Aero cars changed. A front-drive model, the Aero 30, was announced. Its 1 litre two-stroke engine, with needle crankpin bearings, developed 21kW (28hp). The engine, the gearbox and the final drive were located under a long bonnet, which gave the car a sporting appearance. Some car bodies were designed at the Sodomka bodyworks in Vysoké Mýto. The cars could do as much as 100km/h (62mph).

The last Aero cars were made in 1945.

DELAGE D8 1933

Manufactured by Automobiles Delage, Courbevoie, France

The Delage car factory was involved in racing from its foundation in 1903. Even the first single-cylinder car of Louis Delage was entered for races.

After the First World War the company tried to make its mark in the luxury range. A big six-cylinder model with a 1 litre capacity for each cylinder was built. The camshaft, located in the cylinder head, was driven by a vertical bevel drive shaft. However, the car was a commercial failure.

Bigger successes came with races. Delages came 2nd and 3rd in the 1924 French Grand Prix in Lyon, and a year later the outstanding racing driver Robert Benoit won this event in a Delage. In 1927 Benoit won the Grand Prix of Montlhéry, the Monza, and the San Sebastian, making Delate the most successful racing cars of the year.

At the same time, the company kept an eye on the so-called *Concours d'Élégance*, which were popular at that time. At the 1929 Paris Motor Show a new model, D8, was introduced. It had an in-line eight-cylinder 4060 cc engine, with bore and stroke of 77×109mm. The touring version developed 59.2kW (80hp), the sports 66.2kW (90hp). The four-speed gearbox and the engine were one solid block. The rigid front axle was suspended on semi-elliptic leaf springs. The car weighed 1440kg (3175lb).

In 1934 a 12-cylinder Delage won the perfection contest in Cannes, where it was exhibited in a coupé-de-ville version. In 1939, the jury in Monte Carlo was so impressed by the Delage D8/120 that this car, fitted with Villars cabriolet body, almost 5.5m (18ft) long, was awarded the first prize.

In spite of all this success the company suffered from financial difficulties, and in 1935 Louis Delage had to sell out to the Delahaye car factory. Émile Delahaye had been producing up-market cars since 1894 and his company was known for fast motor boats and the taxi cabs it supplied to New York City.

Delage cars were produced under that name even after amalgamation, but both Delage and Delahaye disappeared from the market in 1954.

PACKARD TWELVE 1933

Manufactured by the Packard Motor Car Co, Detroit, Michigan, USA

The history of this trademark begins in Warren, Ohio, where two entrepreneurs, James Ward Packard and George Weise, set up a workshop producing electrical appliances. Young Packard, who was fascinated by engines, soon realized that the future belonged to automobile manufacturing and so he and his brother, William Doud Packard, established a car factory. The first Packard model, Type A, was built in 1899. From then on, a new model was announced every year, designated by a letter of the alphabet.

One of the most famous was the Twin-Six 1915 model. With a power unit based on the successful Liberty aircraft engine, this car was the first American 12-cylinder automobile. It enabled Packard cars to take the lead over high-quality car producers such as Pierce-Arrow and Peerless. It was largely the work of Jess G. Wincenta, the chief engineer, who with his team laid emphasis on every detail of these comfortable cars and devoted much attention to their styling and longevity.

Successful in the tourer class, the company also tried to establish its name in racing. It set a few records with special front wheel driven racers.

The company's speciality was bodywork designed in co-operation with famous American stylists, among them Dietrich, Le Baron, and Brewster, and also individual body building by, among others, Roolston and Waterhouse.

The Packard Twelve model had a 7300 cc 12-cylinder water-cooled V-engine. Cooling was provided by a centrifugal pump and a fan fitted with a thermostat. The car had synchromesh gears and a clutch with a centrifugal booster. The rigid axles were suspended on semi-elliptic leaf springs. Mechanical drum brakes operated on all four wheels. The four-seater had a top speed of 160km/h (100mph). The convertible roof, designed by Count Alexis de Akro Sakroffsky, gave the advantages of a convertible while maintaining the comfort of a limousine.

Packard merged with Studebaker in 1954. The Packard trademark ceased to exist in 1958.

PIERCE-ARROW SILVER ARROW   1933

Manufactured by the Pierce-Arrow Motor Car Co, Buffalo, New York, USA

The New York Stock Exchange crash in 1929 and the period of economic recession that followed did not hamper technical progress. On the contrary, the American car industry generally favoured the idea of producing big, luxurious cars to win back lost profits. So many famous car manufacturers built cars of the largest capacities, fitted with eight-cylinder engines (Chrysler, Duesenberg, Cord), 12-cylinders (Packard, Lincoln, Franklin), or even 16-cylinders (Marmon, Cadillac).

After five years of co-operation with Studebaker, Pierce-Arrow tried again to make its name as a maker of the biggest and most expensive up-market American cars.

Its greatest hit was the Silver Arrow, built for the 1933 Chicago World Exhibition. It had a water-cooled 12-cylinder engine developing 128.7kW (175hp). The car had an independent suspension and servo-brakes. It was offered at $10,000, but did not bring the selling success anticipated, and the five cars produced could not fill the company's half-empty cashbox.

Despite its efforts, Pierce-Arrow could not have made long-term profits with this kind of car. The company — like many other American firms, among them Duesenberg, Marmon and Franklin — did not realize that in order to ensure commercial success, it was necessary to change the car from a luxurious and expensive thing to an everyday utility runabout. The company, facing ever-growing financial difficulties, ceased to exist in 1938.

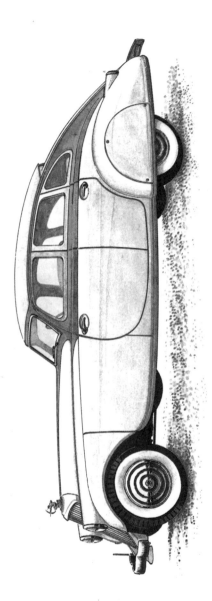

CITRÖEN 11   1934

Manufactured by SA André Citröen, Paris, France

Citröen made the first front-driven production automobile.

In 1934 the prototype Citröen Traction-Avant, fitted with a 1300 cc engine, was introduced under the type designation 7. Its all-steel streamlined body, styled by American bodymakers, did not resemble any contemporary model: for example, it was the first car without the traditional footboards.

Despite the success of the Citröen 7, André Citröen made a new request to the design engineers: 'Cut the Seven into two pieces and make it 12cm (5in) wider! I want to see the prototype in two months!' Sure enough, the new Citröen 11 appeared in July 1934. The first series was still fitted with the 1300 cc engine developing 23.5kW (32hp) which was very little power for a 1-tonne limousine. Therefore a second series with a 1628 cc engine with a performance of 26.5kW (36hp) was manufactured in the autumn; it was followed by a third series with a 1911 cc engine having an output of 34kW (46hp). It was this last version that brought the Citröen success, which lasted until 1957, when the last of the Citröen 11s was manufactured.

The engine, clutch, and gearbox could be removed in one, thus facilitating easy repair. The panel frame, firmly attached to the body, was supported on torsion bars, patented by Ferdinand Porsche. The front wheels were independently suspended. The car, with its elongated body, had a low centre of gravity which ensured excellent road holding.

Because of its excellent driving properties, the Citröen 11 was very popular with gangsters, and in the vernacular it was called 'the gangster car'.

The Citröen 11 was produced mostly as a four-door limousine, but there still exist a few roadster and coupé versions in collections.

HISPANO-SUIZA TYPE 68   1934

Manufactured by Sté. Française Hispano-Suiza, Bois Colombes-Seine, France

In the 1920s and 1930s Hispano-Suiza cars were among the giants of the motoring world, along with Rolls-Royce in England, Maybach in Germany, and Isotta-Fraschini in Italy.

Immediately after the First World War, the company introduced its beautiful model H6 with a whole handful of original construction ideas. The in-line six-cylinder 6597 cc engine with valves in the cylinder head, developed 100kW (135hp) at 2400 rpm. The seven-bearing crankshaft was not forged, as was the usual practice, but turned from a steel bar. The duplex vertical carburettor was controlled from the centre of the steering wheel. The steering column alone consisted of five finely machined concentric tubes, also facilitating the pre-ignition control and the horn.

The chassis was an oblong frame, and the rigid axles were suspended on unusually long leaf springs. The chassis alone weight 1250kg (2760lb). With the body, the car weighed almost two tonnes, and had a top speed of 130km/h (80mph). Such a giant needed servo-brakes. The light-alloy brake drums were ribbed to provide cooling. The reliability of the double ignition was guaranteed by two accumulator batteries.

In 1931, after the merger of Hispano-Suiza with the Société Ballot company, there came the excellent Hispano-Suiza 68 model, which experts still consider to be a king among cars. The square engine with bore and stroke of 100mm had a total capacity of 9424 cc. This well-tried 12-cylinder V-engine was derived from an aero engine, and was the work of Swiss engineer Marc Birkigt. It was rated at 147kW (200hp), which gave acceleration from 0 to 100km/h (0-62mph) in 11.5 seconds. In direct drive, this huge car could reach 170km/h (106mph), but in spite of its outstanding performance it met with no commercial success. The market was orientated towards small-capacity cars after the years of Depression.

DUESENBERG SJ 1935

Manufactured by Duesenberg Motor Co, Indianapolis, Indiana, USA

Duesenberg racing cars earned the company some repute. As early as 1921 Jimmy Murphy won the first French post-war Grand Prix in a Duesenberg fitted with a Miller engine. In 1923, 1925, and 1927 Duesenbergs won the Indianapolis.

After production of the A series — in which Erret Lobban Cord had participated — came to an end, the brothers Fred and August Duesenberg tried to build a huge, comfortable, powerful automobile, which was to be an impressive reply to the demand of rich Americans for the best that the engineers and designers could offer. So a supercar of the J series was designed. *Vanity Fair* journal described this Duesenberg as 'the best car in the world', an exaggerated title which applied to American standards only.

In 1932 the company developed a more powerful model, the SJ (S for supercharged). It had an in-line eight-cylinder 2×OHC engine with four valves per cylinder. It was fitted with a rotary supercharger with which the engine could devlop 235.4kW (320hp) at 4750 rpm. A three-speed gearbox was connected to the engine via a two-disc clutch. The standard chassis was fitted with rigid axles suspended on semi-elliptic springs. The hydraulic brakes, with a vacuum booster, used a water-glycerin mixture. The car had a top speed of 210km/h (130mph).

Fred Duesenberg died in an accident when driving a Duesenberg in the mountains of Pennsylvania. The year 1937 put an end to this independent trademark, and the firm was incorporated into the Cord-Auburn-Duesenberg Company.

August Duesenberg died in 1955. Ten years after his death, Fred Duesenberg Jr. wanted to revive the fame of the family trademark, and built an up-market automobile fitted with a Chrysler engine and styled by Virgil Exner. However, the price was not high enough for the market for which the car was intended. This venture was the swansong of a trademark which in the 1930s represented the highest American technical standards.

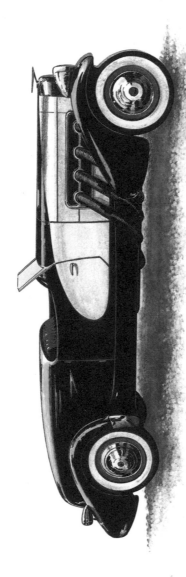

LAGONDA RAPIER   1935

Manufactured by Rapier Cars Ltd, Hammersmith, London W6, England

Wilburn Gunn, who began his career with the production of motorcycles, founded the Lagonda car company in the late 1800s. Up to 1933 the company made only heavy, solid tourers of 3 litres and 4.5 litres. Then it produced a new small sports car, the Rapier 9.5 HP.

The 9.5 HP designation indicated the taxable horsepower. Two camshafts in the cylinder head controlled the valves. The 1086 cc engine, fitted with two SU-type carburettors, was rated at 33kW (45hp) but could be tuned up to 51.5kW (70hp). This super-tuned version was entered for races. The drive was transmitted via a four-speed gearbox fitted with a pre-selector. The chassis had both rigid axles suspended on semi-elliptic springs. The wire-spoke wheels were fitted with hydraulic brakes. With a standard engine the car had a top speed of 120km/h (75mph). In the convertible version the automobile weighed 900kg (1980lb). The roadster pictured here belonged to the few models which had coachwork by Whittingam and Mitchell.

But the Rapier did not bring the Lagonda company the expected financial reward, and production was curtailed in 1937. The balance of orders was taken over by Rapier Cars Ltd., which was established for that purpose, with the former Lagonda designer, W. H. Oates, at its head. The new company fitted the production cars with compressors, and thus enabled owners to enter for races without expensive modifications. This version of Rapier had a top speed of 144km/h (90mph). Altogether 300 Rapiers were built.

The Lagonda company realized too late that it was possible to win commercial success with a small car. The firm was purchased by the Aston Martin-David Brown company, famous for its sports cars, in 1947.

MERCEDES-BENZ 500 K   1935

Manufactured by Daimler-Benz AG, Stuttgart-Untertürkheim, Germany

The Mercedes-Benz 500 K is a classic example of the solid and reliable automobiles of the 1930s. The car was first built in 1934, and was replaced by a more powerful version, the 540 K, in two years.

The 500 K model was fitted with various body types — a roadster, a special roadster, an open tourer, a cabriolet in A, B, and C versions, a sports coupé or a limousine. The bodies differed in the number of seats, side-windows, and doors. Other versions included a streamlined coupé, the so-called 'highway courier', as well as armoured models for high-ranking army officers.

The car was fitted with a 5019 cc in-line eight-cylinder engine. At a low compression ratio of 5.5, the engine developed a power of 117.7kW (160hp) at 3400 rpm. Among other notable construction features were a nine-bearing camshaft, a company-designed duplex carburettor, and a Roots compressor. The compressor was started in third gear at a speed of 30km/h (19mph) and disengaged at 3400 rpm, which coincided with a speed of 100km/h (62mph). It facilitated acceleration only. At a steady cruising speed the semi-automatic Maybach overdrive system was engaged. The frame chassis was fitted with swing axles with balance springs at the rear, and independent wheel suspension in front. The low-pressure tyres were fitted on Rudge wire-spoke wheels.

The operating instructions specified a maximum speed of 175km/h (108mph). An expensive item was that the oil had to be changed after every 1500km (930 mi). Altogether 354 of these cars were built.

TATRA 77   1935

Manufactured by Tatra, Kopřivnická vozovka, as, Kopřivnice, Czechoslovakia

Efforts to build an automobile with a higher performance at a low consumption introduced new trends in car designing. One was streamlining. At the 1934 International Car Exhibition in Berlin there were four cars which could have been said to start the era of streamlined vehicles: the Tatra 77, Chrysler-Airflow, Steyr 32 PS, and a 1 litre DKW.

The prototype of the Tatra 77, which became the first production car with a streamlined body, had an air-cooled V8-engine located behind the rear axle. The engine was easily accessible by lifting the fin-shaped rear bonnet. The gearbox was located in front of the rear axle. Ever since, this arrangement has been used in almost all cars with rear-mounted engines. The frame consisted of a central member and cross-members, which carried a well-styled streamlined body utilizing the whole width of the vehicle. As a result, three people could sit next to the other on both front and back seats. The prototype Tatra had the steering located in the centre of the car, and the seats beside the driver were moved slightly back to provide more legroom and avoid the inner wheel arches. Behind the back seat, between the gearbox, the clutch, and the half-shaft drive, there was a roomy luggage compartment.

The Tatra 77 proved that building an air-cooled engine was no longer a technical problem. The 3 litre engine with bore and stroke of 75×84mm was rated at 44.1kW (60hp) at 3500 rpm, developing a speed of 145km/h (90mph). After the first 100 cars built in 1934, the engine was re-bored to 80mm in order to increase the acceleration, giving a capacity of 3.4 litres. It developed 53kW (72hp). The next batch of 150 cars was produced over the period 1935-1937.

This more powerful Type 87 became famous for a journey around the world, where its performance, reliability, and durability were clearly proved.

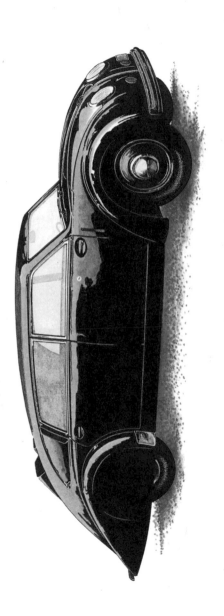

PANHARD-LEVASSOR DYNAMIC   1936

Manufactured by SA des Anciens Etablissements Panhard et Levassor, Paris, France

In 1936 Panhard-Levassor introduced a model which was often considered to be a mere prototype or a unique coachwork study. Yet it was a production car, and from 1937 it was the only car under this name.

Panhard-Levassor was one of the last European companies to adhere to the valveless sleeve-valve engines, manufactured under licence from the American Charles Knight since 1907. Many European firms had fitted their cars with Knight engines, such as Mors, Voisin, Peugeot, Clement, the Belgian Minerva, and even the German and British Daimler. The sleeve-valve arrangement guaranteed extremely quiet running; but it raised production costs, and so many companies abandoned it at a time of financial restraints and ever-growing demand for higher engine output.

The Panhard-Levassor was supplied with two engines of different capacities. The six-cylinder valveless 2.9 litre engine developed 58.8kW (80hp), the bigger 3.8 litre engine 73.5 kW (100hp). The integral body had independent suspension in the front and swing axles with torsion damping at the rear.

The car was notable for its unusual streamlined body of the French school, which emphasized the dynamic features of the car. The curved corner windows were needed because the driver's seat was central until 1939.

Even after the Second World War the Panhard company lost nothing of its progressive approach to car designing. in 1945 a talented designer, J. A. Grégoire, a pioneer of front-wheel drive, developed a prototype small car with an air-cooled opposed twin-cylinder 600 cc engine. Panhard manufactured this economical engine under licence, and used it in a new model, the Dyna-Panhard.

Before it merged with Citröen in 1965 Panhard introduced its last two models, the PL 17 Tigre and Panhard 24 C.

AUBURN 851 SC   1937

Manufactured by Auburn Automobile Co, Auburn, Indiana, USA

Auburn ranks as one of the great names of the American motor car industry of the 1930s. Its cars were not mass-produced, but came in the luxury range.

The original company was established in 1877 by a German emigrant, Charles Eckart. The factory was named after Auburn, Indiana, where it was established.

Eckart's sons, Frank and Morris, at first made twin-cylinder models, but then focused on large capacity four- and six-cylinder engines. However, the cars were a commercial failure, and the factory was turned over to William Wrigley.

The company's situation was improved in 1924 when Auburn was bought by Erret Lobban Cord. At the age of 29, this ambitious entrepreneur became president of an enterprise which incorporated the Auburn, Cord, and the Duesenberg trademarks. He started the Auburn golden era, which included the most successful Auburn, the 851 SC.

The car had a side-valve, water-cooled, in-line 4590 cc eight-cylinder Lycoming engine which developed 84.5kW (115hp), or 110.3kW (150hp) when supercharged. It had an aluminium cylinder head and a cast-iron engine block. Hydraulic brakes operated on all four wheels. The rear axle was driven via a three-speed gearbox and a propeller shaft. The frame chassis was underslung on semi-elliptic leaf springs. The car had a maximum speed of 160km/h (100mph).

The last Auburn model, with a 12-cylinder engine, was produced in 1937. After that, Cord closed the company down.

BMW 328   1937

Manufactured by Bayerische Motorenwerke AG, Munich, Germany

A landmark of BMW production in the 1930s was undoubtedly the successful BMW 328 sports car. The company began making six-cylinder cars in 1934 with the 315, which had a 1490 cc engine developing 25kW (34hp). From this a nice two-seater with a roadster body, the 315 Touring Sport, was derived a year later. In succeeding years the bigger 319 and 319/1 were built, with 2 litre six-cylinder engines fitted with three carburettors.

The same engines were used in the BMW 328. The output of the 1971 cc engine with three Solex carburettors and hemispherical combustion spaces was 58.8kW (80hp) at 4500 rpm. The car had a four-speed synchromesh gearbox. Hydraulic brakes operated on all four wheels. The 328 made its mark in such events as the 1940 Brescia Grand Prix (a substitute for the Mille Miglia) which it won; and the Le Mans 24 Hours in 1939, the Le Mans type coupé which won the Brescia Grand Prix had a streamlined aluminium spider body; its engine developed 73.46kW (100hp), and reached more than 200km/h (125mph).

These were originally production cars designed as utility runabouts with sporting lines. Though not among the cheapest, they represented the highest quality of the German car industry. The 328 was manufactured under licence in Britain by Frazer-Nash.

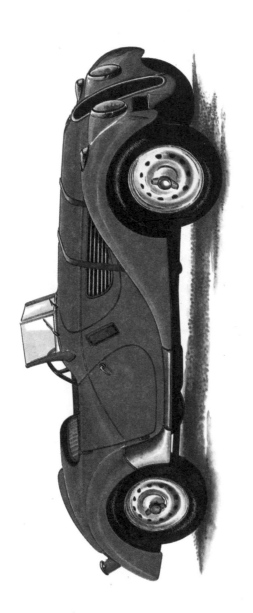

CORD 810   **1937**

Manufactured by Auburn Automobile Co, Auburn, Indiana, USA

Erret Lobban Cord was a shrewd businessman, with progressive ideas in car making. He was certain that a front-wheel drive automobile was a winner. His first effort, the L 29, failed as a result of insufficient power — which made it necessary for the Hollywood stars to use reverse when climbing the steep Beverly Hills. Then in 1935 Cord announced the 810.

This new Cord was based on the L 29. It had a body with a ribbed radiator, and a 3.175m (10ft 5in) wheelbase. Owing to the shape of the radiator the car was nicknamed 'the mobile refrigerator'. The chassis had a split front axle with trailing wishbones, with the gearbox mounted ahead of the axle. The 4.73 litre V8 Lycoming side-valve engine developed 91.9kW (125hp) at 3500 rpm. The four-speed gearbox had an electromagnetic preselector. A notable feature of the almost two-tonne body was the tilting headlights.

In 1936, the engine was fitted with a Cummings supercharger, and in this modification it developed 125kW (170hp) at 4250 rpm. The car was now called the Cord 812. It seemed to be better and cheaper than the ill-fated L 29. But this car was not particularly successful, either. Preparatory work ran into problems, delivery dates were delayed by more than six months, and so contracts were cancelled. Altogether 2320 of these 'refrigerators' had been produced when Erret Cord unexpectedly wound up the whole enterprise.

SS JAGUAR 100

Manufactured by SS Cars Limited, Coventry, England

In 1934 William Lyons, owner of SS Cars, was fortunate enough to engage two outstanding engine designers, William Haynes, from Humber, and Harry Weslake, late of Bentley, and could at last equip his cars with the company's own engines.

Harry Weslake, regarded as one of the greatest engine experts, and 'father' of the Bentley engine, designed a new cylinder head with OHV valve arrangement on the Standard engine, and thus boosted the engine output up to 73.5kW (100hp). This reliable motor became the basis of a new SS Jaguar series. The production programme included limousines and convertibles with 1.5 litre, 2.5 litre, and 3.5 litre engines, and SS Jaguar 100 sportsters with 2.5 litre and 3.5 litre engines.

Its racing successes made the SS Jaguar 100 3.5 litre one of the most famous Jaguar cars. It was the first car of this type that exceeded the speed of 160km/h (100mph). The engine had a compression ratio of 17.5:1. SS Jaguars were successful in races and trials, with victories in the Marne Grand Prix of Reims, the Villa Real International event, the Alpine Rally, the Monte Carlo Rally, and the RAC Rally.

The car in the picture is a two-seater sports of classic design, with a 2664 cc six-cylinder engine developing 75kW (102hp) at 4600 rpm. Two electric pumps provided the fuel supply for two SU carburettors. The car had a four-speed gearbox. The oblong chassis frame had two rigid axles carried on longitudinal leaf springs and damped by friction dampers. The Rudge-Whitworth wheels were fastened by a central nut. The large diameter mechanical Girling brakes could slow the car down from its top speed of 160km/h (100mph).

Between 1935 and 1940 a total of 315 SS Jaguar 100s were made; 117 of them had 3.5 litre engines.

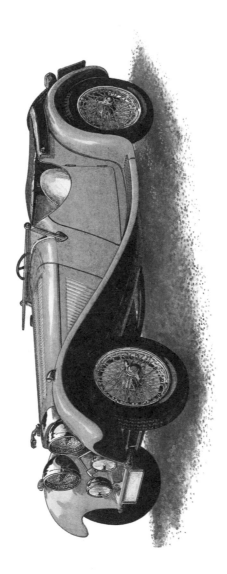

LANCIA APRILIA   1937

Manufactured by Fabbrica Automobili Lancia e Cia, Turin, Italy

Lancia has always been noted for its advanced designs, outstripping contemporary developments, such as the electric starter of the Theta, independent front wheel suspension of the Lambda, and the Superjolle braking control.

The Aprilia, unveiled to the public in 1937, had a streamlined body, the result of the efforts of the designers to increase speed by reducing air resistance. Although the body shape was frequently criticized, it followed aerodynamic principles.

The 1351 cc V4-engine, with the cylinders set at the narrow angle of 17°, was derived from the successful engine of the Lambda. It was water-cooled, with bore and stroke of 73×83mm. The engine block and the cylinder head were made of light aluminium alloy. The valves were controlled by a camshaft set in the cylinder head. The engine developed 34.5kW (47hp). The independently suspended front wheels were supported on coil springs, with telescopic hydraulic dampers. The rear axle employed torsion-bar damping. The Lancia Aprilia was the first car in the world with no lubrication points. The side rods were suspended on rubber bushed pivots, and the front telescopic dampers had automatic lubrication. In order to facilitate access to the passenger compartment, the body had no central pillar. The doors opened in opposite directions. The car could reach a speed of 125km/h (78mph).

The Lancia Aprilia became one of the most popular products of the Turin factory and more than 27,000 were made. Many famous bodymakers, among them Borsami, Bertone, Zagato, Cesaro, Touring, Savro, and Castagna tried their stylistic skills on the quality chassis of the Aprilia.

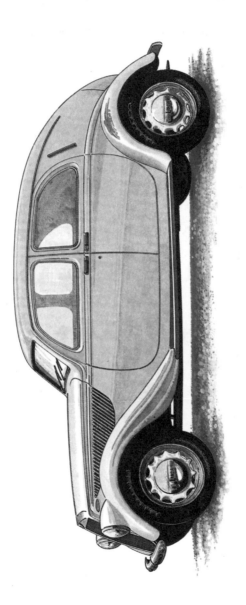

MAYBACH ZEPPELIN 1937

Manufactured by Maybach Motorenbau GmbH, Friedrichshafen, Germany

Being Daimler's associate and the creator of the first Mercedes automobile, Wilhelm Maybach was thoroughly experienced in designing high-performance multi-cylinder cars. After the first victories of Mercedes in various sporting events, the French banker and car enthusiast Baron Henri de Rothschild tried to lure Maybach to France, to set up the best and biggest automobile factory in the world. But Maybach refused.

In 1909 Maybach left for Friedrichshafen on Lake Constance, where he and his son established their own enterprise, Maybach Motorenbau GmbH. It was a sister company to the Luftschiffbau Zeppelin GmbH of airship fame.

Initially Maybach intended to design just engines, and offer them to other car manufacturers: for instance, the Dutch Spyker cars used Maybach engines. But by late 1921 Maybach had built his first automobile. It was the Maybach W 3, with a six-cylinder in-line engine developing 53kW (72hp). The two-gang epicyclic gearbox was designed in co-operation with ZF in Friedrichshafen. The W 3 was followed by the W 5, with a 7 litre engine that developed 88.3kW (120hp).

Maybach made only cars in the luxury range, famous for their big engines and special chassis. The bodywork of his cars was usually made by Karroseriefabrik Spolm. In the 1930s Maybach introduced one of the biggest cars ever built in Germany, the Maybach 12, later known as the Maybach Zeppelin. Its quality, driving performance, and comfort were compared with those of Rolls-Royce. The 12-cylinder 7977 cc V-engine had a rating of 147kW (200hp). The epicyclic ZF-Maybach gearbox had eight gears and, as a curiosity, owing to pre-selection, four reverse gears.

Wilhelm Maybach died in Cannstatt in 1929. The firm was taken over by Daimler-Benz in 1960.

BUGATTI 57 C   1938

Manufactured by Automobiles Ettore Bugatti, Molsheim, France

The Bugatti 57 came on the market in 1934. Bugatti's son Jean did a
lot of work in the car's development. It was made in 57 C, 57 S, and
57 5C versions until 1940.

The first series 57, known as the Normale, was fitted with an in-line
eight-cylinder 3257 cc engine. Two camshafts were located in the
cylinder head. The 100kW (135hp) output at 5000 rpm was
transmitted via a single-plate clutch to a four-speed gearbox. The
valve clearance was adjusted by washers of various thicknesses on the
valve stem. The maintenance manual suggested that 'since the valves
were adjusted only seldom, it was better to send the car to Bugatti's
maintenance shops for a decoke as well'. However, the cylinder head
was not removable, and therefore decarbonization meant taking the
engine completely down. And so, while customers were waiting for
completion of the repairs, they were offered the Italian specialities of
the Hostellerie du Pur Sang, the company's own liqueur distillery
products, and the gallery of works of Rembrandt Bugatti, Ettore's
younger brother.

From 1938 the 57 C was available in a more powerful version fitted
with a supercharger, which gave it 118kW (160hp) at 5000 rpm. The
chassis had rigid axles. The square-sectioned steel front axle was
forged from a single block, with longitudinal leaf springs pushed
through it. The rear axle was suspended on quarter-elliptic leaf
springs. The 57 C had a double-circuit hydraulic braking system. The
standard chassis was fitted with beautiful bodies styled by Gangloff or
Galibier.

Another model of the 57 series, a touring sports Bugatti 57 S,
appeared in 1935. The car had a shorter wheelbase and a more
powerful engine. By increasing the compression ratio to 8.5 and
altering the valve timing, the car could develop 125kW (170hp) at
5500 rpm. The maximum cruising speed was 200km/h (125mph). The
57 S (S for Surbaissé — extra low), with a body styled by Jean Bugatti,
was exhibited at the Paris Salon in 1936. The front wheels were wholly
covered by the mudguards, which turned with the wheels on corners.

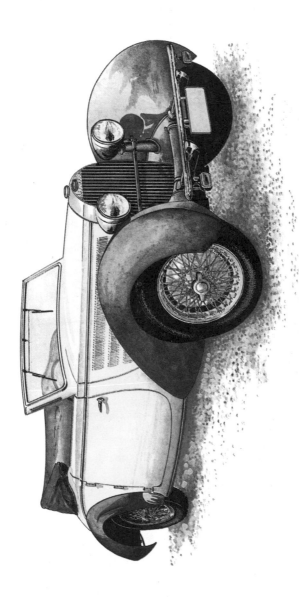

HORCH 951 A   1938

Manufactured by Horch Werke AG, Zwickau, Germany

The Horch eight-cylinder dynasty was started by the 303, introduced
at the 1926 Berlin motor show. It was the first production eight-
cylinder manufactured in Germany. The engine's designer was Paul
Daimler.

From this 3 litre engine others were derived, with the capacity being
increased by 0.5 litre each time, until Horch offered six different
engines which could be mounted on two different chassis types. In the
1930s Horch led in the production of eight-cylinder engines, and more
than 30,000 units were made.

In 1932 Auto Union AG was established. The Horch cars came in the
concern's luxury range — cars with an engine capacity greater than 3
litres.

The 951 A, shown here, was the flagship of Horch's 1938
programme. Under the alumimium bonnet there was a 'chunk of cast
iron', nicely varnished and of simple design. The duplex Soles
carburetor with its air filter and the inlet manifold were on one side, the
exhaust system on the other side. The fan was driven by a shaft
instead of a belt. Both camshafts operated the valves directly, without
rocker arms. The camshafts were driven by a bevel drive. Another
feature was the 'Siamese twin' cylinders, cast in such a manner that
no cooling water could flow between them. The purpose was to obtain
a short engine block. The engine had a small cylinder bore and a long
stroke, and a total capacity of 4944 cc, developing 88.17kW (120hp)
at 3400 rpm. Three of the gears of the ZF four-speed gearbox were
synchronized. The car's weight was another story — the chassis alone
weighed 1850kg (4080lb), and the whole car weighed 2650kg
(5842lb).

These models brought Horch the reputation of being exceptionally
solid, reliable, and elegant.

PEUGEOT 302   **1938**

Manufactured by Société de Automobiles Peugeot, Sochaux-Montbéliard, France

One of the last family enterprises, Peugeot owed its vitality to several factors. These were a specific tradition and deliberate conservatism combined with a flair for novelty, and the proverbial reliability of the cars. The quality of Peugeot cars was perhaps guaranteed by the factory's location at Sochaux, in the Montbéliard region, famous for its long tradition of clock making. There was great loyalty among the staff, and one can find three generations of one family working in the factory. Recurring names like Jean-Pierre I, II, and III suggest royal dynasties.

Despite its conservatism, a detailed analysis of the company showed that Peugeot always introduced their novelties at the right time — when the best sale could be expected.

Such was the situation in the late 1930s when Peugeot presented their new streamlined models. The headlights sunk under the radiator grille, the covered rear wheels and the sleek, flowing rear section limited air resistance and resulted in low fuel consumption and a high top speed. The least-powerful model, the two-door limousine N 2, had a 1333 cc four-cylinder engine and weighed less than 800kg (1760lb).

The N 3 was a five-seater sedan fitted with a 1758 cc four-cylinder OHV engine and a three-speed gearbox.

At the 1938 Paris Salon the model shown here was judged the nicest car exhibited. This stylish four-door limousine was fitted with an air-cooled four-cylinder 2142 cc engine with bore and stroke of 83×99mm. The car was supplied with a manual three-speed gearbox or, on request, with an automatic four-speed Cotal gearbox. With a sedan body it weighed 1186kg (2620lb).

Throughout the company's history its cars had a long production life. The 302 was produced unchanged until 1949.

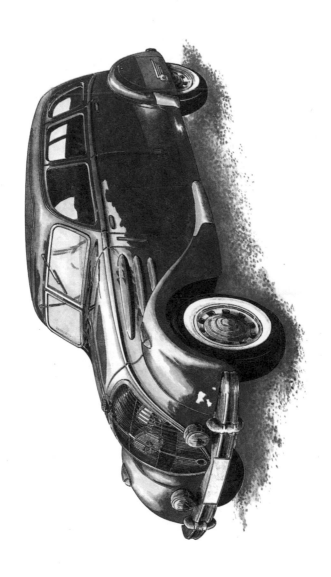

ALFA ROMEO 8 C 2900　　　　　　1939

Manufactured by Alfa Romeo Spa, Milan, Italy

Following the great success of the six-cylinder Alfa Romeo 1750, produced without interruption until 1934, the factory introduced a new car of the same type in 1931 but with an eight-cylinder engine. The cylinder dimensions were the same as those of the previous model — 65mm bore and 88mm stroke — and with two camshafts and a compressor the engine had a capacity of 2330 cc and developed 103kW (140hp) at 5400 rpm. The engine had two cylinder blocks and a two-piece crankshaft. The compressor, the dynamo, and the camshafts were driven by a geared transmission from the centre of the crankshaft.

The 8 C 2300 Monza model of 1931 had an increased engine output of 121.3kW (165hp) at 5400 rpm. This racing version was equipped with separate mudguards and special headlamps. The car was given its name after the victory of Tazio Nuvolari and Giuseppe Campari in the 10-hour Italian Grand Prix at Monza. The chassis of this model became standard for a number of sports tourers, which did extremely well, especially in the Mille Miglia and Le Mans 24-hours.

In 1932 and 1933 Alfa Romeo cars completely outstripped the Bugattis — which until then had been the absolute rally champions — and became the most successful racing marque. Nuvolari, Rudolf Caracciola, Louis Chiron, Luigi Fagioli, and other outstanding drivers won six GP races out of eight and scored victories in the Targa Florio circuit, Copa Acerbo, and other important trials. Alfa Romeo ended up with a clean one-two-three finish in the Reims ACF race and in the German Grand Prix at the Nürburgring.

A more powerful version of the eight-cylinder type, the 8 C 2900, was introduced in 1937. A greater engine capacity of 2905 cc increased the car's output to 132.3kW (180hp) and gave it a top speed of 200km/h (125mph). During the two years it was in production 30 cars of this model were built.

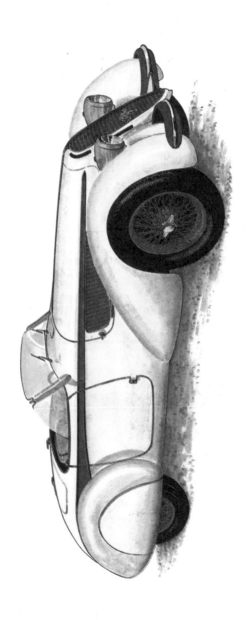

ADLER AUTOBAHN 1939

Manufactured by Adlerwerke Vorm. H. Kleyer AG, Frankfurt, Germany

At the 1936 Berlin Motor Show Adler presented a new sports coupé, notable for many advanced features. The streamlined aluminium body, which today would be referred to as fastback, was mounted to tubular cross-sections, firmly attached to a plate frame. The 1645 cc in-line four-cylinder SV-engine, developing 33kW (45hp) at 4000 rpm, was derived from the well-tried 1.7 litre Trumpf engine, which did extremely well in sports motoring.

After successes in the Le Mans 24 hours and the Spa races, Adler switched from four-cylinders to six-cylinders. The company's Autobahn model, as its name implies, was considered suitable for fast highway driving.

The car, fitted with a 58.8kW (80hp) engine, easily reached a speed of 150km/h (93mph). The side-valve arrangement was quiet at the maximum revs of 4000 rpm. Unlike other Adler cars, this model was rear-driven, though the gearlever jutted out from the dashboard, an arrangement common on Citröen and DKW models. Two, later three, horizontal Solex duplex carburettors were fitted. This large, fast car weighed 1310kg (2890lb).

Both axles were split, contributing to a good road performance. The front wheels were suspended on lever damped control arms and transverse quarter-elliptic springs, the rear wheels were supported on longitudinal trailing arms and transverse leaf springing. Hydraulic dampers and hydraulic brakes operating on all four wheels were standard equipment.

Adler represented the middle range of cars. It never succeeded in joining the group of great German marques, where Horch and Maybach cars belonged, though this was a question of the low prices of the Adler models rather than the quality features of the cars.

VOLKSWAGEN   1940

Manufactured by Volkswagenwerk GmbH, Wolfsburg, Germany

The ingenious car designer Ferdinand Porsche developed the original Volkswagen as early as 1932, during the Great Depression years. Then he sold the working drawings to the NSU company, and at the same time sent a letter with an enclosed set of drawings to the Reich Government. The response of the German Fuhrer, Adolf Hitler, sounded like a command. He asked for a car to accommodate five passengers. The car should be of a sturdy design, fitted with an air-cooled engine running at high cruising speeds on the motorway yet giving excellent performance on country roads. Great emphasis was laid on simple construction to make repairs easy. This was to be the Volkswagen — the 'People's Car' — and cost no more than 1000 marks.

Porsche presented two prototypes, designated as Type 3, at the 1936 Berlin Motor Show. Car producers criticized the body design, and considered the whole conception of the car as much too expensive. Porsche had failed to build the car for less than 1200 marks. So he went to Detroit in order to study the American motor industry and mass-production. In America he purchased machine tools, presses, and automatic machines.

Finally the foundation stone of a new factory was laid on May 26, 1938, and the first series of 20,000 cars was produced in 1939. The Volkswagen was fitted with a rear-mounted air-cooled four-cylinder flat engine with a capacity of 1131 cc developing 17.8kW (24hp) at 3000 rpm. A fan forced the air stream against the cylinder ribs. The oil cooler guaranteed good oil lubrication, so the car could be driven at a cruising speed of 100km/h (62mph). The four-speed gearbox was built in one with the final drive. The Volkswagen's frame was pressed from steel plates. The front axle consisted of two rigidly connected tubes containing leaf torsion bars. The swing axles of the rear wheels were anchored by wide arms, joined with adjustable torsion bars of circular cross-sections. Damping was provided by double-acting telescopic dampers.

The Volkswagen became known as the 'Beetle' because of its shape. It remained in production until January 19, 1978, by which time 19,200,000 cars had been built — even more than the legendary 'Tin Lizzie'.

INDEX

222